YOU
DON'T
KNOW
JACK

KEVIN D. CORDI

UNIVERSITY PRESS OF MISSISSIPPI / JACKSON

YOU DON'T KNOW JACK

A STORYTELLER GOES TO SCHOOL

The University Press of Mississippi is the scholarly publishing agency of
the Mississippi Institutions of Higher Learning: Alcorn State University,
Delta State University, Jackson State University, Mississippi State University,
Mississippi University for Women, Mississippi Valley State University,
University of Mississippi, and University of Southern Mississippi.

www.upress.state.ms.us

The University Press of Mississippi is a member
of the Association of University Presses.

First printing 2019

∞

Library of Congress Cataloging-in-Publication Data

Names: Cordi, Kevin, author.
Title: You don't know Jack : a storyteller goes to school / Kevin D. Cordi.
Description: Jackson : University Press of Mississippi, [2019] | Includes
bibliographical references and index. |
Identifiers: LCCN 2018041314 (print) | LCCN 2018044492 (ebook)
| ISBN 9781496821263 (epub single) | ISBN 9781496821270 (epub
institutional) | ISBN 9781496821287 (pdf single) | ISBN 9781496821294
(pdf institutional) | ISBN 9781496821249 (cloth : alk. paper) | ISBN
9781496821256 (pbk. : alk. paper)
Subjects: LCSH: Storytelling—Study and teaching—Anecdotes. | Drama
in education. | Storytelling in education. | LCGFT: Informational works.
Classification: LCC LB1042 (ebook) | LCC LB1042 .C497 2019 (print) |
DDC 808.5/43—dc23
LC record available at https://lccn.loc.gov/2018041314

British Library Cataloging-in-Publication Data available

TO MY LOVING WIFE, BARBARA. WITHOUT HER,
MY STORY WOULD NOT BE AS COMPLETE.

CONTENTS

ACKNOWLEDGMENTS

I am indebted to my mother and father, Mr. and Mrs. Lyle and Ota Cordi, who taught me my first stories and continue to teach me every day the value of living life well.

I thank Dr. Amy Shuman, whose continual sage advice helped me further acknowledge the relationship storytelling has for the academy and beyond. Your belief and care in my work are deeply appreciated. Dr. Brian Edmiston not only expertly shared with me the wonder and educational value of process drama but also changed my teaching and how I listen and respond to my students. Dr. Patricia Enciso showed me the value of sociocultural learning and reflection. I value these people not only for lending an ear and eye to my research, but for shaping me as a teacher as well. I value their wisdom and friendship.

I am grateful to Elizabeth Snell, who edited my work. Our continual friendship is a document that will last. Anthony Hoehn's second look at this work enabled me to make it better.

Thanks also to Mr. H. Glenn Allen and Mrs. Jean Allen, whose continual support is long lasting and appreciated.

Last but not least, I acknowledge my students, my fellow storytellers, and my teaching colleagues, who helped me have topics worthy of reflection. Because of you, the stories continue to be told.

YOU
DON'T
KNOW
JACK

CHAPTER ONE

YOU DON'T KNOW JACK
A STORYTELLER LOOKS BACK

I am a storyteller. For the last twenty-seven years, I have toured as a professional storyteller all over the United States and beyond. I know the value of placing students in a story trance as they listen to an African folktale where the trickster Anansi struggles to find how he can own all the stories of the world. I have regaled kids and adults, sharing how my dog Jack delivered papers with my brother Mike but had to stop because the customers complained their papers arrived wet. Perhaps Jack should not have carried them in his mouth. Nothing can replace that experience. This was not my only work. For fourteen years, I also taught high school in three schools in Ohio and California, carefully designing lessons so students could create meaning. For many years, I kept these worlds separate. In my early teaching career, I did not share how I was raised on West Virginia stories because they were not part of the curriculum. I had separate identities, teacher and teller. However, that trickster known as "story" was not settling for these identities to be in just one place. Story insisted on an invitation to my classroom, and I invited it in. Once it was there, it stayed, but I wrestled with how best to use it. How would I change when I blended teller and teacher into both arenas? How would I balance these worlds, or should I seek to balance them?

I attempted to sustain the engagement between my worlds: that of teacher and that of professional storyteller. However, sometimes these worlds don't flow together. I was raised on stories from Appalachia. I felt that my mother's stories, although they taught me a great deal, were not welcomed in the classroom. Still, I could see them slowly being applied in my teaching. It took time, but my voice as teller, teacher, and student of Appalachia became a tool of my classroom. I often felt the community I was working with wanted one voice, but I wanted to have many voices. My identity contained a single voice, until I began to refine, reflect, and re-evaluate the use of voice and story in each setting. In this book, I explore how my identity has shifted as a storytelling teacher. In doing so, I release, revisit and ultimately redefine how I use what I know about story and drama. I examine how I use storytelling, storymaking, and drama as systems of learning instead of simply ways to entertain students. I show how stories are used and do more than record; I critically reflect upon the use of storytelling and storymaking, with and without the use of drama, in order to inform my future work as a storytelling teacher who wants to promote inquiry and learning. I do so by writing as a means of reflection. I do this by providing both a window to my work and a mirror to reflect on how these identities have influenced and continue to influence my understanding of how narrative operates in and out of a classroom setting.

Denzin (2008) states, "The goal of autoethnography . . . is to show rather than to tell and, thus, to disrupt the politics of traditional research relationships, traditional forms of representation, and traditional social science orientations to audiences" (69).

In one sense, this work can be considered an autoethnography, but I am not sure that it should be confined to this category. What I do know is that this is more than the telling of a story; instead it is a critical reflection of not only my work but the work of others and how these stories influenced and troubled my thinking. My autoethnography is a story relating my life as it structures my teaching practices. By writing about how I understood what it meant to be a professional storyteller and writing to guide my thinking, I can critically reflect on and learn from my experiences. My writing allows me to examine my past coupled with my present.

Learning from this work as much as re-visiting it, I want it to produce a personal transformation. I hope it will change me as an educator, instead of being torn from my artistic and teaching identities; I will create a new middle as a new understanding of what it means to have multiple identities when teaching. In her book, *Nepantla: Essays from the Land in the Middle* (1993), Mora reflects upon her discomfort of living on the borders, between the United States and Mexico; between European-American culture and her own Chicana culture:

> There probably isn't a week of my life that I don't have at least one experience where I feel that discomfort, the slight frown from someone that wordlessly asks, what is someone like her doing here? But I am in the middle of my life, and well know not only the pain but also the advantage of observing both sides, albeit with my biases, of moving through two, and in fact, multiple spaces and selecting from both what I want to be part of me, of consciously shaping my space. (6)

I, too, have asked myself both as a storyteller and as a teacher, "What am I doing here?" I have also heard these questions asked by others. From shaping my space in the many worlds in which I live and work, I am in a new middle, but in this middle grounding, I need to look back to see what lies ahead as I work with storytelling, story-making, and drama to improve as a teacher.

First, we must learn from a boy named Jack. Jack lived with his mama, and one day his mama told him, "Jack, it is time to seek out your fortune." Although Jack was reluctant, he set out to find what he could find . . .

Every culture has stories and with them storytellers. Within the tales of the teller lie accounts of both wise and foolish actions. In particular, in the Appalachia and British regions, there are numerous tales about a boy named Jack. The most noted tale is "Jack and the Beanstalk" or "Jack and the Bean Tree," but other tales abound of this often mischievous and wise folk character. There is "Jack and the Northwest Wind," "Jack and the Robbers," "Hardy Hard Head," and "Jack and the Heifer Hide." Although these tales reach homes all over the world, they were not the stories shared around my home when I was a child. Still, I am Jack. Instead of telling Jack tales, my mother would recount her own tales of growing up in West Virginia. If one listened close, they were similar to the exploits of Jack. My parents introduced many of the traditional Jacklike tales to my five brothers and sisters and me as we sat on a dilapidated old couch in Ohio. The stories followed the Jack motif—a young, poor boy (girl) would leave his or her family to find something new, becoming tempted along the way and often discovering something more of the journey. This boy or girl would transform in some poignant way as a result of his or her travels.

My folks were poor. The Jack tales appealed to them. The traditional Jack tale is not the story of nobility, but instead is a common tale. My father worked at Goodyear Tire and Rubber Company in Akron, Ohio, and, due to his disability, often was without work. He struggled to feed his family and to avoid long stays at the hospital. However, he pressed on. Like Jack, despite the obstacles, he continued. Sometimes Jack's reward was sacks of gold, a kingdom, or the hand in marriage of a princess, but other times the rewards were internal, such as gaining friendship, advice, or awareness. My father regaled us with stories, and often this was our reward. In his stories, he taught us how to live or question the world. I remember him telling me that when he worked at a Coca-Cola bottling plant and had to use the bathroom, his boss said no, but he did anyway. In so doing, he stopped the entire bottle line. He was fired, but the next day, he was rehired with an apology. We all have human needs, and we should fight for them. Jack is constantly fighting for these human needs. After all, we could understand a poor boy wanting more than he had. This is our story. Jack tales are not steeped in the tales of kings and queens, but, instead, in the ordinary person's journey, my story. It is hard to remember when I first heard tales like these because they were part of our daily life. As much as we watched television, my mother, and sometimes my father, would still take time to tell us stories. Octavia Sexton, who tours the country telling Jack tales, shares in this experience: "Ask me to remember when I first heard these stories is like trying to remember when I first had a drink of water, it is impossible. I don't know. I just know there was a time we heard these tales and told them" (Wolf 2010). Although these Jack tales have their roots in Britain, they changed when they landed on American soil. The Jack tale not only has become an American tale but is also emblematic of an American journey. As Lindahl (1994) notes, when Jack came to America, his journey changed: "The American tales—perhaps like American Culture in general—foreground the individual, but not without offering him a social order that ensures his success" (xxxi). The individual highlighted in Jack tales is Jack, but Jack does not roam around aimless; he has a sense of order. Jack follows rules. Often one does not understand Jack until he explains his actions. He can and often is foolish but not without direction. He tries to seal the northwest wind because he is cold, and, as a result, even though it sounds foolish, he does it. The order that he follows does not come from a kings' decree or from being an inherited part of royalty, but instead it comes from the rules of an individual—lying will hurt you, the journey is one you must take, and sometimes saying nothing can go a long way. It is a common journey. It is Jack's journey. My story is a Jack journey.

Jack is pervasive in American culture. As McCarthy and Stotter (1994) note, simply hearing the name Jack rings with Americans. Jack is in our lexicon. Stotter and McCarthy state, "Jack, according to the dictionary, is a generic name for any representative of the people. Jack is one of the folk, an everyman figure" (154). I also represent an everyman story. As I mentioned, I too am Jack. In my journey to be a storyteller, I ventured by myself to discover what this means, to find my fortune. At first, my journey was not to explore being a storyteller, but instead becoming a disc jockey, but along the way, like Jack, I had magical teachers to guide me. I was transformed and instead became not only a storyteller, but a "story teacher" (Gillard 1996). This rich, almost mythic pursuit has both troubled and informed me. Like Jack, I wrestled with finding my path, but as a result of being lost, I found new direction and in turn expanded what it meant to be a storyteller and an educator.

This story begins in the American classroom. As a high school teacher, I did not realize that story could assist me in my teaching or that story was another form of teaching. I found this by accident. Once I discovered how story could be used as a meaning-making tool for students' learning, I began to question how storytelling and storymaking can further address how students can learn with narrative tools and serve as pedagogy. Then, as a university professor, I further expanded how story acts in an interactive way to create meaning and began to advance a narrative pedagogy, incorporating process drama and narrative dimensions. Like Jack, I made my share of mistakes along the way and continue to do so, but as a result of those mishaps, new direction was formed. I have also explored story in new ways in and out of the classroom. I have served as a national consultant in more than forty states, England, Japan, Singapore, Scotland, and Canada, and most recently, Qatar. However, with every step, I learn more about my Jack journey. He started unsure and even unwilling to begin—his mother had to throw him out. When he had to begin this personal journey, a new awareness formed. Like Jack, who would finish one quest only to begin a new one, I embark every day exploring new ways to use narrative. I continue to test and retest what I know about this art called storytelling and how it changes when it is used for teaching. This is why the Jack story serves as the perfect metaphor for my discovery of what it means to be a storyteller on the road, in the classroom, and in the halls of academe.

I was raised on the tales of Appalachia. I, too, was a poor boy, a mere youth of nineteen when I discovered organized storytelling. I was accustomed to my mother sharing tales, but not others. I found storytelling on a fall day at Kent State University in Ohio. I did not set out to be a storyteller; storytelling found me. Jack was waiting for me like he was there for renowned Jack teller Ray Hicks: "That's the way it was when I growed up. When you git like I tell it, I'm Jack. Everybody can be Jack. I've been Jack. I mean in different ways. Now I ain't everything Jack has done in the tales, but still I've been Jack in a lot of ways. It takes Jack to live" (McCarthy 2010, 5). Jack is in all of us. His story is about acting on desires or needs, even if one does not want to. There is a personal Jack journey that we must take.

Jack teller Octavia Sexton agrees: "I heard stories that people call Jack tales. When I was growing up and we were telling and listening to stories we didn't use the name Jack. Maybe Jack was in a tale or two, but we used the name of someone that was a well-known name, like a family name because I grew up listening to these stories" (Wolf 2010). I was not looking for Jack, but it took a Jack tale to direct me toward my vocation, to help me find my direction. At eighteen, I left for Kent State University to be a disc jockey similar to Casey Kasem or Rick Dees, popular deejays at the time. I enjoyed listening to music and sought a life sharing music with the world. However, the real work of a deejay was not always exciting since the radio station gave me a midnight shift. It was work, and work that I did not always want to do. Until storytelling arrived on campus, I was lost. As it is often with Jack, he wanders, and people and places guide him. He will simply be taking a walk but finds a princess on the way. I no longer wanted to spin records; instead, my head was spinning with uncertainty, looking for direction. The needle of this path kept skipping. I needed to find something or someone to help me. The people or animals who help Jack often provide him with magical items like a picnic blanket that has unlimited amounts of food, but only if you can say the secret words. I did not encounter magic beans or meet a stranger named "Drink Well," but my fellow students assisted me with whom I was and whom I could become. Like Jack, I needed to leave home to find meaning in my life. This is the first stage in my journey. In fact, Sobol (1992) states the Jack tale represents a series of stages in life. He says, "Jack as a matter of fact, is less of an individual character than an emblem of human potential in many of its representative stages" 15).

Jack represents the journey seekers we can become. As de Lint reminds, "the spirit of Jacks of old is in you. It's a lucky name—as the tales that your people still tell can vouch for" (119). As a storyteller, I needed to recognize that Jack resides in me. Texas professional storyteller Mary Grace Ketner (2013) notes that a Jack tale chronicles the journey of every person. She notes that Jack can be called Hans, Anansi, Brer Rabbit, or simply a traveler seeking more than the road can offer. In these tales, Jack exemplifies both the foolish and the wise choices in all of us. This work chronicles the wise and foolish choices I made on the path to become a storyteller and also highlights the challenges and promises of being a storytelling teacher. As a teacher, one of the foolish choices I made was limiting the stories I allowed in the classroom. It took a while to realize a storytelling teacher is more than a person who tells stories, but, instead, is someone who uses stories as a primary means of teaching. I slowly realized that story could be used not only for performance, but also to promote inquiry and engagement with and for students. Initially, I saw the role as someone who told stories, but over time I learned to think and respond using narrative. This heightened what it meant to be a storyteller and story teacher. When students confronted me with issues, I turned to stories and storymaking to guide my advice and instruction. This was not a quick or easy journey. First, I had to recognize the importance of my past to understand my present pursuit.

I was raised on journey tales. My mother nurtured me and my five brothers and sisters with her stories carrying us back to her hometown of Clay County, West Virginia. However, I did not realize that she was doing this. I thought I was simply hearing a good yarn. In fact, her vivid descriptions shared in our place in Ohio transport us to Appalachia, on an old wood porch. Here her tales began. With each tale, we learned more about her search for her fortune. Along the way, people like our mother taught stories to her that contained advice such as how to can food for the winter so they could survive. Stories of hardship became guideposts for living. She had nine sibling brothers and sisters, and they needed guidance. Stories were the compass for living. My mother would share hard-time stories, but also tell stories about eccentric family or "kin." Her sister, my aunt, Ruby Starcher, acted as wild as a black snake in the Clay County holler when the two of them got together. She would account for the rumbles with "the boys"—her brothers, Ed, James, Homer, and Dude. Her stories also spoke of compassion in difficult times. She told of Wavey's store, where if one didn't have any money for penny candy, Wavey always slipped a surprise in the bag when the child was not looking. At her mother's small house, even though they could afford little, they did not turn people away when they needed a place to sleep. They couldn't afford a fancy tutor, and because of distance and weather or need for chores to be done, they often did not attend school. Story became my mother's teacher, and she, in turn, shared this with us. Each tale my mother told was to teach my siblings and me about living. At that time, I learned what it meant to listen to stories, but it would be awhile before I told the stories, and it would be even longer before I understood the teaching that could develop from telling and making narratives. However, like Jack, sometimes you have to experience life to know your next or your true direction.

My Jack journey challenges my identities as teacher, storyteller, and student wrestling with who to be and when to be it. It does not contain a beanstalk, but it is about growing and discovery. Initially, for example, I did not think folk- and fairy tales could be incorporated into the high school classroom. My educational training did not prepare me to use narrative as a means of teaching. Storytelling was what I did away from school—entertaining children primarily—that was separate from my goals as an educator. What place did a fairy- or folktale have in a senior literature class? I questioned this until Jack stepped in. Jack was not expected to step into the college classroom at Kent State University, where I trained to be a high school teacher. Jack generally was not a common figure striding the hallway of Brunswick High School in Ohio as I prepared lessons on *The Canterbury Tales* or the proper way to provide a persuasive speech. Although we began to use stories, he came in one step at a time. I slowly developed a story curriculum and began using folktales gradually as I realized the value of stories and my role of a storymaker and teller. As Jack Zipes (2012) states, "For once a plethora of stories began to circulate in societies throughout the world, they contained the seed of fairy tales, ironically tales at first without fairies formed by metaphor and metamorphosis and by a human disposition to communicate relevant experiences" (4). The experience of my students and my own stories were not integrated into my teaching. Jack did not have a welcome mat even though he and Jacklike stories of struggle and reward were all around my classroom and school. His did not arrive until mid-year in 1995 when a young high school freshman named Jennifer Wooley asked me to create a storytelling club, Voices of Illusion, after school. How was I to know that this was the beginning for me to develop and use narrative in new directions? At that time, I also began to realize that essential to storytelling was listening, deep listening. This was the framework of story. But still, story arrived, and, being the trickster he is, *The Canterbury Tales* became the Brunswick Ohio tales, and students continued to tell stories. However, sometimes I did not listen deeply to my students' stories. Instead, the prescribed curriculum artificially implanted itself over the rich narratives of my students.

I was not always the listener. In the corridors and the hallways, my students told stories. I told them to stop telling stories so we could begin our work. Little did I know that these stories could be, and often were, the work. They shared account after account with each other. However, as a teacher, story was separated from the curriculum. How could teachers teach simply by telling a story? Herein lies my journey of what happens when story comes to school. How does the school environment change when storymaking and storytelling are the primary tools for learning? Like in *The Canterbury Tales*, the journey provides answers, if not spaces for learning how to value narrative as a teaching tool. This is a journey of fourteen years as a classroom teacher, eleven of them teaching storytelling at the high school answering to the moniker of "the storytelling teacher." It is reflecting both as a high school teacher and as a university professor on how I could have better applied storymaking and telling in the classes.

Jack arrived at a time when curriculum was prepackaged and state mandated. It often still is as long as we accept it. The form of assessment was not in the narratives of my students but found in rubrics and formative and summative assessments. In many places and at this test-driven time, it still is. How was I to add telling and making stories in the mire of mandatory requirements? Story was not required or expected. Story is a trickster; when I was not looking, the students told stories, and it was the students who reminded me of its importance. They achieved better when sharing their narratives. In recounting this experience, I need to rely on more than my story. Many other contributors such as my parents, students, and teachers helped me learn the words.

I did not realize the influence old family stories and folktales would have on me and who I am today. My mother's stories, like the old English ballads "Barbara Allen" or "Taffy was a Welshman," served as our nightly entertainment. It was similar to Ray Hicks's experience: "When I was growing up, that's all the entertainment we'd have, a tellin' stories. When us youngins would git together and git a little rough, somebody would start one of them (Jack) tales. One would take a part, and all of us kids would quiet down and you could hear a pin drop" (McCarthy 2010, 4).

Living in Akron, Ohio, I could not be the mountain teller; I did not identify with this title. I did not live near a holler, and I was many miles from West Virginia. As a kid, I was raised listening to mountain tales, but I felt more like a fan, not an insider. It was like a window to this world, but not a door. I could look in, admire what was there, but stay on the outside as I leaned in to see more. I was awestruck from watching what was going on inside. I could listen and be an ear to my mother's stories. We could hear tales such as the time when the blind Fuller Brush salesman Walter Hayes arrived at my Grandmother West's home carrying a big brown suitcase, selling vanilla, Geritol, kitchen tools, horse liniment, utensils, and salves when my grandmother lived in Big Otter. He staggered into each piece of furniture, and my grandmother mistook him for a drunk. When he asked for something to eat for the road, my grandmother fed him "hard-as-rock biscuits" known as chicken bread, which are said to be so hard "you could knock a bull in the head with them." The salesman quickly left. We would laugh, as my mother would share that from that day on my grandmother earned the reputation as a "sorry cook" because as the salesman traveled from door to door, he never failed to share the story of the biscuits that he could not eat. I was not the storyteller, and I did not live in the mountains, but through my parents' recollections, the mountains became clear. I began to know, understand, and connect to the mountains because mountain people shared their tales. It was a slow process, but, over time, as I heard the tales and as I asked questions, I proudly began to claim my Appalachian roots. However, this was, as I mentioned, a slow development, but stories shortened the road to knowing. Before that, I wondered, how could I call myself Appalachian if I was not born in parts most known as Appalachia?

My parents were from the mountains, and I was not. Because we not only heard of and rarely saw the mountains except for an annual family trip, how could I call myself an Appalachian story-teller? Although my parents referred to themselves good-naturedly as "hillbillies," they were careful when they identified as someone Appalachian or hillbilly.

I witnessed this recently at a storytelling festival in Akron, Ohio. At intermission, my mother stood behind West Virginia storyteller

Suzi Whaples, and when Whaples turned around, although they had never met, she hugged her and said, "Come here, you dirty hillbilly." Suzie gave her a big hug and called her sister. I realized then being from the mountains meant that you have an entrance into the mountains. However, place too had its value. Where you were raised could make a difference in determining your degree of quality of your Appalachia status. I shared a book of poetry from a West Virginian poet, and after reading it, my mother stated, "The author is not from my mountains." It was true; she did live in a more urban community of West Virginia. My mother did not connect to her story. It was clear that one must reside and speak from a tone that she recognized in order to authenticate the title of being West Virginian.

What it meant to be Appalachian or an Appalachian storyteller was not formally shared with me, but others, including my parents, were quick to share who was or who was not allowed to take this title. Perhaps telling Appalachian stories was a key to this world. I recently told stories in a different part of West Virginia sharing mountain tales I had heard as a child. I distinctly remember one listener, an older gentleman, who said, "We don't tell those mountain tales anymore. They are from the other side." When pressed, I was told people used to live that way, but soon after, two people privately took me aside and said, "We still do," and winked at the secret between us. In contrast, when asked to tell stories in Clay County, where my mother was raised, during their Golden Delicious Apple Festival, I was welcomed because I had the language of invitation. I knew the place because my mother had taken me there with her stories.

As far as the tales of the mountains, initially I listened but did not tell them. My brothers and sisters might ask for our favorite tales, but it was in the listening that we learned how to live. Little did I know that in a few short years the roles would reverse, and I would research and tell stories to my students.

I never saw myself as a teller when I was a kid, but I did love stories. Jack too was raised on mountain ways. He is emblematic of my life direction. As Sobol illustrates, "Generally speaking then,

Jack has become a sign in English for everyone, and beyond that, for the male principle in any of its lowly or earthly expressions" (Davis 1992, 17). I needed to leave my comfortable surroundings to discover what was outside of my home. This too was true of Jack: he left, or his mama threw him out, so he could discover his own way of living. At one point, I tried to leave mountain ways, only to discover that it was hard to quit how you were and are raised.

I didn't always cling to the mountains. Like many teenagers, I wanted to run away from my roots. I would be more likely found in a Pat Benatar shirt with a chain wallet than be seen at a Bluegrass festival. Still, country music ran rampant in our house. Music permeated the walls, recordings of Conway, Cash, and Owens, mixed with the Billboard Top 40, and as my father yelled "Turn the junk off!" I was often forced to choose country music. I hid my interest in other music. By day, I was listening to ACDC, but by night I was listening to "Tight Fitting Jeans." The weekly shows hosted by Barbara Mandell and later, the *Johnny Cash Show* were "must sees" for our little television. At home, I was glued to the box, watching Conway Twitty, George Jones, and Loretta Lynn. At school, I was immersed in Dungeons and Dragons and hard rock. As a teen, I struggled to understand my place. My mother would sing, "Give Me that Old Time Religion," but, at the same time, I would tape the top forty songs on the radio and yell out, "Take those old records off the shelf!" At the time, I felt twisted and restricted, but, despite the struggle, I had an appreciation for each direction.

The narratives of my childhood served as a springboard to my education. During my four years at Kent State University studying new methods of teaching, story was not part of the process. Later, I found myself returning to stories told on that old, used couch in Akron, Ohio. As a high school teacher and then university professor, I value the teaching methods I use and story, but stories also work to create meaning. As much as stories are a form of discourse, I now view teaching and learning as conversational narratives that occur within and without the classroom. Working with story led to questions and acting on that inquiry, and effective teaching was a result. It was the interplay of the narratives that produced results. This work will share how narrative is an interactive way to learn. It is about my search to understand what this means and to refine it so that I truly can own the moniker of "storytelling teacher." This American storyteller hopes that other teachers find their own Jack in their classroom and from reading the narratives set out to find their fortune. As Sexton reminds, "Jack is alive and well and he does not just live way back in a long time ago, he lives right next door" (Wolf 2010). He is in the here and now. He serves as my guide, and I hope he finds you too.

In this work, I share my discomfort and mishaps, and detail not only my new awareness but also my direct teaching approaches used to enrich my understanding of narrative use in the classroom.

Rather than stating facts or arguing claims, I use narratives that were emotional, passionate, and situational about my research and experiences within the classroom to travel back to reveal and discover arguments and suggest improvements. Written from the mind and heart, I want this work to be evocative. The goals of evocative writing are "to encourage compassion and promote dialogue" (Bochner and Ellis 2002, 749). In this case, the dialogue is internal, but when recorded, it becomes an external discovery of my work within the classroom. This internal conversation improves my teaching using story and drama. I draw not only from my voice, but also from my writing. I hear the voices and influences of my students, colleagues, and fellow researchers. Tying my reflections and research together forms my understanding.

CHAPTER TWO

DEEP LISTENING TO STORIES

My storytelling experience began with listening. I sat at the feet of my mother as she shared what it meant to be an Appalachian using story to convey the importance of this identification. However, my identity as a storyteller began to form when I left home and realized after attending the Once upon a Time Storytelling Festival at Kent State University that I too could be a storyteller. After this experience, I wandered aimless as a young adult for a little over a year trying to find storytelling culture in Ohio or simply a place to tell stories. When I did, every teller I met was forty-five and older; no teller was nineteen, my age at the time. I learned again by listening to these older tellers and soon found out that younger tellers were hard to find across the nation. At the same time, I set out to find my fortune—to learn what it meant to be a storyteller. I was on a journey to be a teacher.

I thought in order to be an educator I had to leave the journey of being a storyteller behind, but soon I discovered by accident that saying "Let me tell a story" was an effective classroom management tool. Being from a big family, I was used to noise, but in my first job as a teacher, my freshmen students did like to talk, and trying every classroom management tool that I studied in college did not ebb their off-task conversations. When students were engaged in loud talking, I said, "Let me tell you a story," and they stopped to listen. They didn't only stop; they actively paid attention. They had a natural tendency to listen to stories. It was as though this was a trigger remembered from childhood when narratives help students imagine, escape, and reflect. It was a time that telling and listening to stories was not questioned. They didn't hear stories much as high school teenagers, and from the attentiveness to the invitation, I knew this was something I would continue to use. I used story initially to gain attention, but soon discovered more methods to use it to teach.

For twelve years, I served as a full-time storyteller and credentialed teacher of story-related classes. In fact, the National Storytelling Network (NSN) named me the first full-time high school storytelling teacher in the country because of my daily work, innovation, and commitment to story. I taught classes on introductory and advanced storytelling, creative writing through creative telling, science fiction and fantasy, and drama. With my English and reading assignments, I used narrative as a primary means of teaching. This included designing and teaching a specialized reading class, Rap and Read—Using Oral Language to Teach Literacy, and, for nine years, Opportunity, a class for students labeled as "disadvantaged," created for students as a last chance before dismissal. My unique perspective as a storytelling teacher allowed me to build an innovative curriculum. Over the years, I have been able to experiment, design, and reshape this narrative-based curriculum and tailor it to meet the needs of my students. I became one of the youngest touring tellers in the nation. All of these experiences have helped me become the teller/teacher that I am.

I engaged in narrative research. When working to define the type of narrative research, I turned to the work on the methods that speak to narrative as a way of making meaning and as a method to capture experience. I found it difficult to pinpoint narrative methods that informed my work. Instead, I found value in many narrative perspectives. Due to the interdisciplinary nature of narrative studies, no definitive theory, no paradigmatic definition of what a narrative actually is (Ryan 2004).

In this chapter, I will outline some of the methods that I examined as I wrote this book. The first method I examined is autoethnography.

Autoethnography recognizes that story does more than entertain or retell an experience. According to Jones, Adams, and Ellis (2013), "As our stories illustrate, autoethnography creates a space for a turn, a change, a reconsideration of how we think, how we do research and relationships, and how we live" (21).

Autoethnography is less about telling your story and more about the reflection of what is discovered by framing story within an analytical lens. It does not displace the author's view of the world, but, in fact, it depends on the author's accounts to create the work. Carolyn Ellis eloquently describes this powerful qualitative method:

> Autoethnography is not simply a way of knowing about the world; it has become a way of being in the world, one that requires living consciously, emotionally, reflexively. It asks that we not only examine our lives but also consider how and why we think, act, and feel as we do. Autoethnography requires that we observe ourselves observing, that we interrogate what we think and believe, and that we challenge our own assumptions, asking over and over if we have penetrated as many layers of our own defenses, fears, and insecurities as our project requires. It asks that we rethink and revise our lives, making conscious decisions about who and how we want to be. And in the process, it seeks a story that is hopeful, where authors ultimately write themselves as survivors of the story they are living. (Jones, Adams, and Ellis 2013, 10)

Writing down these experiences invites me to reflect in what ways they are significant. I can look at where narrative worked and where it did not. I can learn from the narrative episodes that I chronicle about the teaching experiences. For example, I can examine the effect when I told a tall tale called "The Gasoline Cat" to a group of kids, but what happened when I did more than tell the story? What happened when I instead had the students co-create it with me? Did this heighten the experience, or was something missing as a result of this involvement? Writing my reflections in a real sense helps me revisit the experience, not simply to see it again but to learn from it.

I can examine how I used stories not only from this experience but the many times when I took risks in my story development.

As a researcher, a new awareness arrives when one examines how stories are used to create meaning. As Mitch Allen (2006) states, an autoethnographer must

> look at experience analytically. Otherwise [you're] telling [your] story—and that's nice—but people do that on Oprah every day. Why is your story more valid than anyone else's? What makes your story more valid is that you are a researcher. You have a set of theoretical and methodological tools and a research literature to use. That's your advantage. If you can't frame it around these tools and literature and just frame it as "my story," then why or how should I privilege your story over anyone else's I see 25 times a day on TV? (8)

In telling the story of my work as a storyteller and story teacher, I use many voices. In fact, I am struggling with these voices. It is not simply the stories contained in this chapter that are the important ones, but it is also my reflection upon these stories that creates significance. The stories serve as transitions in my thinking, pauses in my reflection, and complete changes in my teaching. I attempt to sustain the engagement between my worlds. In this case, I am looking at how to engage between the world of my parents and the world of academia. This is one source of multivoiceness. The reverse is that my parents do not feel engaged in my academic world. Although academic language is distant and remote, through her narratives, my mother reminds me of the significance of my place in learning. This serves to be a powerful lesson in the classroom because of the many voices that reside there. I need to value each voice, my voice as the teacher and my students in the classroom. This includes more than the voices that come from the content that I am teaching, instead, open up the classroom to hear my students. Their own narratives of struggle, living, and questioning have a place. My own stories, learned from my mother, have a place too.

However, I was taught content from texts were the value; I have to learn to value, appreciate, and use student voices both in my teaching and in my telling.

My mother's stories are personal, and still they teach me. Rather than stating facts or arguing claims, I use narratives that are emotional, passionate, personal, contextual, and situational about my research and experiences within the classroom to travel back to reveal and rediscover arguments and suggest improvements. Written from the heart and mind, I want this study to be evocative. The goals of evocative writing are "to encourage compassion and promote dialogue" (Bochner and Ellis 2002, 749).

The reader should realize that unlike other scholarly texts that hide the use of the word "I" when writing and reflecting, autoethnography calls for it. Richardson (2000a) states,

> Autoethnographically based personal narratives are highly personalized, revealing texts in which authors tell stories about their own lived experience, relating the personal to the cultural . . . In telling the story, the writer calls upon . . . fiction-writing techniques. Through these techniques, the writing constructs a sequence of events . . . holding back on interpretation, asking the reader to emotionally "relive" the events with the writer. (11)

In this work, I discuss my teaching experience, not in chronological order, but in order of significance. I consider an experience significant if it allowed me to pause or rethink my teaching or telling methods. Such experiences are worth reflection because they break the routine or the reflex choices of my teaching. When I paused or felt discomfort teaching, I was forced to recognize that other teaching choices needed to be made. When this was happening, I became uncomfortable. I needed to accommodate these changes. This work allowed me to recognize the need to change the way I used stories. It helped me transition from being a professional storyteller to finding new ways as a teacher to plan and teach using narratives.

Another method that I drew upon in informing this work is narrative inquiry. The term was coined by Connelly and Clandinin (1990) for an article in *Educational Researcher*. They view education as the construction and reconstruction of "personal and social stories of teachers and learners (Kim 2016, 18.) In other words, they value the stories of teaching. They state, "Narrative is the phenomenon studied in inquiry. Narrative inquiry, the study of experience as story, then, if first and foremost a way of thinking about experience. Narrative inquiry as a methodology entails a view of the phenomenon" (2006, 477)." These researchers support when teachers study how narratives work and why they do or do not work, educators begin to understand ourselves better as teachers. In this work, I use the rich stories of my teaching and the students and how they respond to foster further inquiry into my work as a teacher and teller. For example, when reviewing my classroom practices, I draw on the stories of my students. These are the stories that we have told, such as a new way of looking at *The Canterbury Tales* or further exploits of Jack. However, when looking closely how I applied drama to address an inquiry question such as, "Could we survive a fall off a mountain?" I examine the stories that unfold because of how we addressed these questions. As Daiute (2014) states, "The power of narrative is not so much that it is *about* life but that it interacts *in* life" (xviii). Narrative inquiry is a search to understand what happens when we use stories, not simply record events.

I discovered this method in 2017 when I was selected to participate in a conference on the *currerre* method at Miami University. Under the direction of Miami University professor Tom Poetter, educators learned that the *currere* method, which is often used in education, implements narratives to understand teaching experiences.

However, this method concentrates on the past work of teaching to inform the study. This method recognizes that by looking at the past and reflecting on these experiences, we are informed about current practices. In order for this reflection to occur, it must happen on a continual basis. In 2017, Pinar, the founder of the method, states, "The Latin infinitive of curriculum—currere . . . is to empha-size the experience of curriculum, lived embodied experience that was structured by the past while focused on the future" (1). He (1978) also states, that it is achieved "through conscious work with oneself and others." This work depends on continual reflection of my students, their stories, and my use of stories with them. It is continual and constantly reviewed by me.

Currere highlights the lived experience. This is why in this work I do more than tell my story; I share more about why the stories were used and not used well. What was I missing out on? Where could I have improved in the storytelling and storymaking? I emphasize my curriculum as a storytelling teacher and also as an artist or sto-ryteller and how they connect and do not connect how narrative is or is not used for teaching.

I review and reflect on the significant moments during these times. These reflections provide me directions that I did not explore in the past but now can consider as I critically examine the how and why I made narrative choices in the classroom.

This teaching story is one of promise and discovery, though it chronicles my struggles and personal change. There were many times I questioned if storytelling was the most effective method for learning. There were other times when my students surprised me with the complexity of their story development and the risks they took because of the safe environment we had created for shar-ing. This work speaks to the comfortable accounts in the classroom using story, but also the discomfort I felt experimenting with using story and story-making drama. I struggled to change who I was as a teacher and performing artist. It is about the direct contrast and compliment learned from being raised on Appalachian storytell-ing. This helped form my identity as a storyteller. Sometimes, my expectations as a storyteller directly conflicted with my established identity as a teacher.

Identities are not fixed categories, like "I'm Appalachian." Rather, in some contexts, my Appalachian identity becomes significant, and in others, it does not. This is why storytelling is so crucial for identity. We tell stories about who we are. We tell stories to help explain our experiences to ourselves. Narratives provide meaning to experience. We sometimes reject the narratives others impose on our experiences. As Baumeister and Muraven (1996) argue, "it is obvious that identities do not come into being into a vacuum. Nor do they emerge first and then merely seek out a suitable context for themselves. Thus, societies can play an important causal role in creating and shaping identity" (405). Sometimes my personal identity as a storyteller was in conflict with my collective identity as an educator. My collective identities of storyteller and classroom teacher sometimes were in conflict. One way to recognize my many identities was with narrative. As Keller-Cohen and Dyer (2000) note, narrative helps one reveal how narratives change in our lives: "In contemporary scholarship it has become commonplace to observe that speakers use the site of narratives to construct particular identities . . . the construction of identity being understood not as a single act, but as a process that is constantly active, each telling a story offering the narrator a fresh opportunity to create a particular representation of herself" (150). However, before the narratives are constructed, one must understand what they are and how they act. In the case of my teaching identity, sometimes the storyteller expectations were the ones I adhered to when teaching my students. However, there were times this was not the most effective teaching choice. At these times, I sometimes struggled with the choices I needed to make and chose my storytelling identity over what a teacher should do or could do to improve learning. This critical reflection is about the difficult, sometimes abrupt or gradual transformation and blending of my identities. My understood and misunderstood identities as storyteller, drama teacher, and process drama specialist had established rules, and in order to improve my teaching, I learned to challenge their tenets. As a storyteller, I learned to see stories as valuable in the ways they were told. As Stone (1997) points out, "Storytelling in all of its contexts is a dynamic experience in which participants assume social identities as tellers and as listeners." Stone goes on to say that these identities are more "rigidly defined than in casual telling" (233). Sometimes, I would bring my storytelling identity into my work in the classroom. A similar effect occurred when I was teaching drama. As a drama teacher, I saw using drama as a privileged art, used only by those studying theater. As an educator, I argued with which identity supported my students' learning. I asked myself questions like the following: Is a storyteller approach appropriate for the classroom teacher who uses stories? As a theater-trained teacher, how could I possibly use drama outside of my formal training arena? In wrestling with such questions, I was looking to change my teaching because I not only learned, but also experienced, new uses of story (storymaking, process, and dramatic inquiry), beginning to question my teaching choices.

In writing this book, I am also searching for where I was troubled in my teaching. I continue to shift who I was as a teacher to who I am now. I use stories to learn from my own teaching and storymaking and storytelling. One might say I am learning between my work as a storyteller, storymaker, and teacher. I am searching for a "new middle" (Pratt 2008; Welty 1984). In Chicano literature, this is called *nepantla*, connoting in-between or the space of the middle (Mora, McKnight, Ceballos, and López, 1993). Anzaldua (1999), a social theorist and activist, addressed issues of identity creating states of in-between different "realities." These in-between realities can be compared to my work as teacher and storyteller. After all, we are storied people (Clandinin and Connelly 2000). In these storied worlds, we search to find meaning for our actions.

From birth, humans are agents in a storied world, where their actions and intentions are understood through narrative structures. Narratives are used to keep track of the regularities of one's own existence and to make sense of strange, new experiences (Davis, et al. 2008, 47).

Most of all, this work is about transformation. How have I changed as a teacher during my fifteen years in public schools, as a storyteller in the classroom, and most recently as a teacher who uses dramatic inquiry to help students learn? I have become a different teacher as my identities and understandings have shifted, changed, and ultimately reformed. In fact, when two identities are in conflict, a new one is formed. Mora, McKnight, Ceballos, and López (1993) call this a "new middle." This is where I am; I am in the middle of what it means to be a storyteller who works in the classroom. I am in the center of my understanding of how to use drama for learning. I stand between my work as a professional, performing artist, and as a teacher. In this study, I seek more understanding as to how these identities work in concert and sometimes in conflict within the classroom. I endure a personal transformation in order to become a more informed and skilled teacher. I look to transform my understanding so it improves my teaching. "Personal transformation however, involves an internal power struggle between the deep yearning for growth within you and those seemingly insurmountable forces that desire to keep you where you are. Forces whose muscles have been strengthened and toned by years and years of habit of incorrect thinking and action" (Nyabadza 2003, 1). I continue to shift who I was as a teacher to who I am now. I use stories to learn from my own teaching of storymaking and storytelling.

This study debunks some of my formal training as a teacher. My educational preparation included coursework as a classroom teacher where I was expected to create lesson plans accounting for each minute of my instruction. Using stories and drama, there were times we did not follow a timed schedule; instead, we followed our collaborative inquiry. Each day's stories built upon the prior day's discovery, as we simply explored a question or subject, spending time researching and developing narratives or using drama to study within the fictional world. Time was not measured in physical intervals, but instead by what was significant for my teaching. In these reflections, I examine what the students were learning or not learning. I question how I plan for instruction as a teacher.

My assumptions about storytelling developed from years of training as a professional storyteller and were echoed and reinforced by a community of storytellers. Many of the people I worked with had limited time in the classroom because they were invited into the classroom as guest artists only. As a teacher, I had my own classroom. I built community daily within my classroom and used stories for longer projects such as exploring *The Canterbury Tales*. Instead of reading the tales, we made our stories based on mixing their lives from the frames of the tales. I was both teacher and artist, but a teacher who was first using artistic understandings and skills to teach as I was performing. I am always a "storyteller, story teacher" (Gillard 1996). However, I still followed storyteller assumptions in my dual classroom role. This study troubles these assumptions as I work to become a better teacher. I examine points of discomfort—times when it seemed awkward to teach under these assumptions.

1. Told stories are privileged as tools for learning. As a storyteller, I learned stories must be told in order for them to be considered "valuable." In many of my assignments as a teacher, my students created stories, but only to be told. The creative process of storymaking was to serve as the result of telling. This work examines the storymaking process as a valuable part of learning.

2. In order for a story to be performed, it must follow a prescriptive method. Stories that are told must be told in a certain way. This usually consists of students sitting in semicircles sharing stories while the teller stood and shared the tale. This was the "standard" telling environment. In fact, many storytellers insisted on this environment before they shared their stories. I question this formula and present new environments for both storytelling and storymaking.

3. No questions are to be asked while a storyteller is telling a story. I followed this for years. It was the classroom expectation. In fact, I often treated storytelling time as sacred time. Questions were not asked until the story experience—the telling of the complete story—was finished. This work examines what happens when students are not only allowed, but also

encouraged, to ask questions about the stories while they are shaped, told, and/or shared.

4. Storymaking only serves to promote storytelling. As I discussed earlier, I privileged storytelling over storymaking. I did not examine how the actual narratives that were shared as stories were made. The questions, the involvement, and the diversity of responses were not examined as much as the telling. This work allows me to reflect upon the student learning during the storymaking process.

5. A told story must have a beginning, middle, and end in order to be shared. I often told students they could not share their stories unless they had these essential elements (Collins and Cooper 1997). This work allows me to look not only at stories that have these components, but also the messiness of stories (Pagnucci 2004) when shared as fragments or incomplete thoughts. This reflection allows me to examine story fragments as teaching techniques. This includes holding back part of a story to increase interest.

In order to examine these assumptions, I "bend back" (Guralnik 1982, 45) and critically reflect upon my experiences in the classroom, using story and drama for teaching. However, I do this not as a journal to recount my experiences, but instead as critical reflections that will provide me a method to weigh my comfort and discomfort as a teacher over the years. This is different than standard writing. It is more than memoir. It is a critical reflection that incorporates many voices, including my own, to examine my practice. Gergen and Gergen (2002) also eloquently state, "In using oneself as an ethnographic exemplar, the researcher is freed from the traditional conventions of writing. One's unique voicing—complete with colloquialisms, reverberations from multiple relationships, and emotional expressiveness—is honored" (14).

Readers respond to this voice. As I write about my past experiences, I draw upon my new understanding of using stories and drama from my doctoral work at Ohio State University. There is a personal change that comes from writing to form a "new middle" (Pratt 2008; Welty 1984). For me, writing becomes a powerful tool

to not only address my many identities with teaching and performing, but to produce change as well. Welty (1984) understood this.

> Writing a story ... is one way of discovering sequence in experience,
> of stumbling upon cause and effect in the happenings of a writer's own
> life ... Connections slowly emerge. Like distant landmarks you are
> approaching, cause and effect begin to align themselves, draw closer
> together. Experiences too indefinite outline in themselves to be recog-
> nized for themselves connect and are identified as a larger shape. And
> suddenly a light is thrown back, as when your train makes a curve,
> showing that there has been a mountain of meaning rising behind
> you on the way you've come, is rising there still, proven now through
> retrospect. (90)

Through retrospective writing, I intend to help shine a brighter
light on my teaching practice. Sometimes, like a neglected room,
teaching experiences will stay dark because no one has entered in a
long time. In the middle of my teaching experience, I did not make
time in an organized fashion to record my reflections; instead, I
simply learned new methods by doing them. As I write, I construct
myself, and in so doing, I begin to understand my actions. At the
same time, understanding my motivations informs what I write and
how I make meaning (Richardson 1997). I look closely at the narratives that occur from my experience, rather than through them.
Richardson speaks to the value of authentic, yet critical, writing.

This work is concerned with narratives in two interrelated senses:
making stories and telling stories. "The act of composing a narrative is a tool for making sense of some aspect of the world, and the
resulting narratives are used to frame one's knowledge. Narrative
is both means and an end" (Davis, Sumara, and Luce-Kapler 2008,
45). Storytelling is the actual telling of stories, which, in my past
teaching, was the only product or result I was interested in pursuing. However, storytelling always involves storymaking. In my identity as a professional storyteller, I previously did not highlight the

educational value of the storymaking process. In this work, I examine not only the use of told narrative to create meaning for students, but also how students construct meaning or create narratives. For example, a student may tell a story about Christopher Columbus. The student works to make his story accurate so he researches and spends time with the teacher designing what he wishes to perform. There is learning involved in the process. The interactions between students and teacher allow students to test ideas and learn how a story is constructed. Students are able to distinguish what parts of the story are significant for telling. By creating and telling this "told story," the student telling and other students listening can raise questions about the story, and they may tell additional stories in response.

This book is also concerned with how I define performance as it relates to learning. Is it necessary to perform stories before a listening audience, or can stories be part of an experience in lieu of a structured performance? The more familiar definition of performance is connected to the way a storyteller shares a polished story for a listening audience. However, as I have discovered, performance can occur even in classroom conversations. As Bauman (1978) asserts, a story is performed once it is uttered. This work explores this definition of performance. It addresses whether students can be inside the narrative as opposed to performing it? How do and can I employ performance in my teaching?

In this study, I record and highlight those times when I stepped away from my traditional teacher training, including times I taught English or drama. For example, as a theater teacher, my training and practice, which included Summer Stock Theater in Kentucky, showed me how the theater operates. It directed me to understand that my classroom should be or could be a microcosm of the theater world. As a theater teacher, my goal was to prepare students for a possible theater career or at the least, to understand how to behave, perform, or learn from the professional theater. I learned and taught the importance of auditions, rehearsals, and script reading. Whereas I privileged told stories in my storytelling classes, I privileged the training and performance or "try outs" of actors in my drama classes. The best roles went to those who worked for them.

This study also reflects my changing understanding of how drama can be used in classrooms to promote learning. In contrast with drama as theater performance (i.e. drama as a product), I focus on drama for learning and the process of using drama in the classrooms. I use O'Neill's (1995) term "process drama" to refer to classroom drama focused on learning. I also use Edmiston's (2010) term "dramatic inquiry" to refer to process drama pedagogy that highlights learning through inquiry. As I developed a deeper understanding of process drama and dramatic inquiry, I let go of some of my assumptions about drama as theater in order to understand other ways of using drama to engage more students and promote learning.

A key teaching assumption that I challenge is that the teacher is solely responsible for knowing and leading the curriculum. I began to learn the value of negotiated learning, listening more to my students and working with them, and even at times, having them help me build my curriculum. In Heathcote, Johnson, and O'Neill, *Collected Writing on Education and Drama* (1984), Heathcote shares that teachers should "negotiate with significance" (25). What is meant by significance is to take a specific view instead of a general one. She states, "The teacher must be able to take a significant view from a general one, and make it happen with meaning to those who bring it into focus" (32). In a speech, Heathcote (1978) also shares that a teacher's perception must also be significant.

> All these things make them pay attention. But there's something a bit odd about saying to children, "I'll create this depicted world so that you can pay attention to it." Children often don't have experiences to make that work. And so, we need the skill of high-level negotiation to help the classes we work with pay attention when we try to distort matters into significance for them. To do this we have to be able to create significance, and we cannot do this if we teach casually. We can only create moments when children stumble upon an authentic

experience if we teach with attention to detail and its relation to the whole. This is the root of excellence.

I note the times when instead of imparting my curriculum, I shared the process of learning by inviting my students to help me shape and even challenge the curriculum. The students' actions and language helped me change what we were doing in order to advance the learning using stories and drama. As I highlight, the teaching choices I made to negotiate classroom learning changed me from authority figure to mediator of learning.

CHAPTER THREE

EXPLORING NARRATIVE

I am concerned not only with the textual definition of narrative and the stories created, but also with narrative as a mode of communication that operates in an interactive fashion. There are many ways people have looked at narrative. I am interested in how narratives work with students when they are constructing meaning through storytelling.

I am primarily interested in an interactive approach to narrative, that is, people engaging in continual communication as they share ideas through storytelling. For students, storytelling is one way of co-constructing meaning out of experience. In his now classic essay on how narrative works, William Labov (1972) describes narrative as "one method of recapitulating past experience by matching a verbal sequence of clauses to the sequence of events which (it is inferred) actually occurred" (396). This seemingly technical way of understanding narrative is useful for understanding how narrative works. Labov explains that narratives are not always told in the same order as the events they describe. Instead, narrators "recapitulate" the past; they reconfigure the order of events to make meaning.

As Rosen (1988) observes, narratives are not as simple as a "neat match between experience and a sequence of clauses" (10). The match is never exact. Labov, other sociolinguists, and folklorists studying conversational narrative have pursued these ideas further to understand how narrative works in everyday interactions. Folk narrative research includes both textual comparative studies of

tales collected from particular cultural groups and studies of traditional storytelling performances (Mills 1990).

Recent years have seen a shift to narrative studies in education
and social science. This research relies less on text and more on use:
context of performance. "As a fundamental genre that organizes
the way in which we think and interact, narrative encompasses an
enormous range of discourse forms, including popular as well as
artistic genres. The most basic and most universal form of narrative
may not be the products of poetic muse, but of ordinary conversation" (Ochs and Capps 2001, 185). Ochs and Capps (2001) view use
as a significant element of narrative. Hardy (1963) states from studying how narrative is used, "we understand how it is the 'raison d'etre,'
why (narrative) was told and what the narrative is getting at" (12).
In other words, when we study narrative, we learn how and why it
is used. As mentioned, work on storytelling until the second half of
the twentieth century focused not on the interaction involved in
narratives, but on the actual content, the text, itself.

When we think of narrative, literary forms come to mind as narrative texts par excellence. At least since Aristotle's *Poetics*, narrative
genres such as tragedy and comedy have been the preoccupation of
philosophers and critics (Ochs & Capps, 2001, 185).

Over the past decade or so, the analysis of narrative in the social
sciences has shifted away from an exclusive interest in content.
"Analyses of narratives focus more on the ways in which storytellers and the conditions of storytelling, shape what is conveyed as
on what content of those stories tell us about people's lives" (Elliott
2005, 42).

Storytelling and storymaking are primarily concerned with how
people communicate, including listening and telling. How narratives
are performed is becoming increasingly important to researchers
such as Langellier and Peterson (2004), who turned their attention to
the performance aspect of storytelling: "The intervention shifts analytic focus from story text to storytelling performances as embodied, situated, and embedded in fields of discourse" (2). Narratives

found in conversation are called, "performance narratives" (3). The mere act of "let me tell a story" creates a relationship between storyteller and listeners as audience so that "the telling of a story is a performance" (2). However, I wonder if stories are performed when uttered, could stories shared in everyday conversations also be a form of performance? If true, this allows me to rethink how storymaking could be an integral part of performance. Viewing all stories uttered as performance, Langellier and Peterson (2004) believe students working in small groups sharing ideas, often in the form of narrative exchanges, are performing within these exchanges. "As a human communication practice, performing narrative combines the performative 'doing' of storytelling with what is 'done' in the performance of a story" (2). Each communicative utterance could be seen as a performance of stories.

The research on conversational narrative provides a new perspective to my ideas about storytelling; I see storytelling, not simply as a performed practice art before a listening audience, but instead as accepted everyday classroom conversations as narrative performances to examine the learning contained within them.

While students can be entertained by a told story, within the context of a classroom, the primary reason for told stories is to help construct story for students to learn from experience. Storytelling as replaying is one way to see storytelling as learning. The experience is personal; Goffman (1974) views narrative as personal replaying that serves to recount the event. However, not everything can be replayed. Narratives are prone to replaying.

A tale or anecdote, that is, a re-playing, is not merely any reporting of a past event. In the fullest sense, it is such a statement couched from the personal perspective of an actual or potential participant who is located so that some temporal, dramatic development of the reported event proceeds from that starting point. A re-playing will therefore incidentally be something that listeners can empathetically insert themselves into, vicariously experiencing what took place. A re-playing, in brief, recounts a personal experience, not merely reports on an event. (Goffman (1974, 504)

The storytelling experience is more than re-telling, it is a way for students to see again a story or an idea not simply as a past action, but instead as an active experience for learning. Goffman (1974) shows recounting or using narrative serves to personalize experience. He states that the person telling the story allows us to visualize and experience it. According to Smith (2006), speaking about Goffman, "The storyteller recreates the informative state and understanding as they appear at the time so as to vicariously place the listener in the position." (62)

In *Living Narrative*, Ochs and Capps do not concentrate on performed narrative (what I also call told stories), but instead examine stories in the context of everyday conversations, often the same type heard on a back porch or shared informally at a storytelling festival. They are interactive, involving people talking with one another and including narratives as part of talking. They outline five dimensions of narrative: tellership, tellability, embeddedness, linearity, and moral stance. These dimensions can occur in varying degrees. For example, a told story by one performer can have low tellership because only the performer is telling. However, when a group tells together, it creates high tellership. The dimensions work in concert with each other as well. Significantly for this study, stories can appear as fragments; fragments can be neglected, questioned, changed and extended into longer narratives that may (or may not) be shared as told stories.

Keeping use in mind, Ochs and Capps (2001), note, in everyday conversations, people tell stories. Some appear like book texts, displaying basic plots with a clear beginning, middle, and end, but still some others are fragments, neglected, extended, shared, and/or discarded.

This is not to say "polished" narratives are to be overlooked but that there are more narratives to be used for teaching. "Ochs and

Capps don't want to ignore smooth traditional narratives or pretend they don't exist; they want to broaden the framework that includes them so that we don't forget the messy end of the spectrum, the more frequent one" (Agar 2005, 26).

Especially interesting are incomplete narratives or what Ochs and Capps (2001) refer to as narrative fragments. As a storyteller, I believed narratives necessitated a clear beginning, middle, and end to indeed be classified as narratives. These definitions informed my practice with both storytelling and storymaking. According to Ochs and Capps, each narrative, whether finished or not, is a narrative. They claim these fragmented narratives are often more interesting to study. They invite additional interlocutors or active participants to help them discuss or problem solve with narratives. Story fragments are not often found in performance narratives, which are strictly prepared and performed for audiences.

Ochs and Capps (2001) distinguish between everyday narratives and more formal performed narratives, identifying everyday narratives as stories one might hear on a back porch often delivered in fragments whose direction and exchange are often unpredictable. Performed narratives are planned, designed to meet a certain audience's ends, similar to those heard at a storytelling festival. An audience must be present to hear the crafted, performed stories. They further discuss everyday or living narratives: "Living narrative focuses on ordinary social exchanges in which interlocutors build accounts of life events, rather than on polished narratives . . . [M]any of the narratives under study . . . seem to be launched without knowing where they will lead" (2). As Bauman (1978) and Langellier and Peterson (2004) note, conversational narratives are performed in different ways than polished narratives. The very nature of being spoken to as a listener includes "both performance and performativity" (2). In other words, they are performed, but the conventions for performance, including taking a longer turn at talk or following up on something someone else has said, are part of the participants' shared understandings of appropriate social interaction (Shuman

1986). There is a more formalized performance, such as stories told
at a storytelling festival, and less performed events, such as a club
meeting. As Rosen (1986) points out, the narrative is in the making. In other words, speakers shape the conversation. The way the
words are delivered and the environment in which the narratives
are shared contribute to how the narratives are heard, understood,
questioned, and performed. These questions are extremely useful
to me as a performer examining my own performances whether
on stage or in the classroom. For example, in the classroom, I can
consider how participants negotiate the rights to tell particular stories in particular occasions. The same type of narrative lives within
the classroom as in porch-style narrative exchanges. Stories from
the classroom consist of both living and performed narratives; both
involve performance. In my reflection of how students co-construct
meaning using stories, the work of Ochs and Capps (2001) is especially useful for identifying the positions of students and teachers
in the classroom and their use of both performed and living narratives, as well as the distinctions across drama forms, storytelling,
and storymaking.

In the classroom, students talk not only about the work they do,
but also about their personal lives. As noted, narratives are considered performed when expressed, but they can also be seen as texts
or told stories. In this sense, they act as a noun, but also as a verb.
Viewing narrative as performative enables me to see how students
create narratives and use them to learn. In order to further understand how storytelling and storymaking are performative, I turn to
the work of Bauman (1978), who views narrative as an interactive
relationship between what is said and the way an event is formed:
"Performance re-situates narratives as an object of study; narrative is both a making and a doing." He also says, "Literary theorists
occasionally look outward from the texts toward the relationship
between narratives and the events they recount, whereas anthropol-
ogists tend to look in the other direction, toward the relationships
between the narratives in which they are performed." Thus, when

narratives are vocalized, they are performed. Narrative as communication is "situated, its form, meaning, and function" (3). However, these narratives do not all act the same way. Some are provided greater emphasis because of the speakers' privilege, or others are embedded within specific contexts. For example, a teacher could share a story like a storyteller, and because of her authority, she is expected to be the one with the authority to tell stories. Her tellership is high. She has the right to tell. It is expected because of her position in the classroom with the students. However, at any time, if another teacher might tell something considered more important, he might have more tellership. Tellership, in this case, is tied to authority. Narrative serves this function; it can be regarded in the form of degrees, high and low depending on what is being done. By studying these degrees or what Ochs and Capps (2001) call "dimensions of narrative," one can see more clearly how narratives are actually used in the classroom.

Using narratives is about being messy; it is a "healthy disorder" (Ochs and Capps 2001, 181). As noted, narratives are sometimes shared in fragments or whole segments, or they are dropped, neglected, and/or advanced by other stories. In this healthy entanglement, there is a concerted effort to make meaning among the active participants in the narratives. This works on multiple levels for the speakers and listeners in their larger classroom inquiries. Ochs and Capps (2001) outline five dimensions of narrative that can vary in their intensity and significance from high to low: tellership, tellability, embeddedness, linearity, and moral stance. The dimensions can change as quickly as midsentence and can all be operating at the same time. In order to understand how these narratives work, they must be seen in relationship with other narrative dimensions. Performed narratives have traditionally held privilege in the classroom setting over everyday narratives. One might see delivering a lesson plan as delivering the story of the class. There are expected roles of teller and listener when a teacher is presenting or performing the lesson.

Ochs and Capps argue that conventional narratives have privileged one end of that continuum, in particular, one teller instead of multiple tellers; high tellability instead of low tellability; detachment from the surrounding activity at the expense of embeddedness in the local context; a certain and constant moral stance over an uncertain, fluid and dynamic one; a close temporal and casual open-endedness and/or spatial organization (Ochs and Capps, 2001; Georgakopoulou 2006, 238).

However, these dimensions change when more tellers are involved. In order to understand how they change in classroom narratives, one needs to examine each dimension.

TELLERSHIP

Tellership measures a teller's involvement within a conversation narrative, as "the extent and kind of involvement of conversational partners in the actual re-counting of a narrative" (Ochs and Capps 2001, 24). In essence, tellership is about when particular people orchestrate their involvement in the telling of stories. Tellership levels can vary. An example of high tellership is, "on one end of the continuum, the storyteller holds the floor during the unfolding of the tale, while the audience's role is typically to listen attentively" (Ware 2006, 45). Another example is when the teacher controls how much telling and listening can be introduced with and for the students, and depending on the teacher's choices, will determine the tellership in the classroom. High tellership includes a "primary teller" or "set of active tellers" as co-constructors of the stories (25). When more tellers are added, the tellership increases, and they can be involved in the conversation because the narratives are shared. This also raises the opportunity to negotiate the stories. As Dyson (1997) states in discussing informal storytelling in primary classrooms, "composers are not so much meaning makers as meaning negotiators who adopt, resist, and stretch available words" (4) As tellers' co-author stories, they help co-construct the making of the narratives. "The idea of co-construction has been examined as a new way of examining narrative and steering away from the distinction of the active teller and passive audience" (Norrick 2000a, 133). Tellership forms within a classroom context where the teacher is usually seen as the person with sole authority. However, when using storytelling and storymaking and introducing drama, teachers can play different roles and thus create greater tellership for and with the students.

TELLABILITY

In order for narratives to have tellability, they must be reportable. However, listeners can alter the tellability by changing it within everyday conversations. This thought is mirrored by Foucault (1976): "The agency of domination does not reside in the one who speaks (for it is he who is constrained) but in the one who listens and says nothing; not in the one who knows and answers, but in the one who questions and is not supposed to know. And this discourse of truth finally takes effect, not in the one who receives it, but in the one from who it is wrested" (62). Narratives that have low tellability invite other stories to be part of the narrative because they are part of the communicative exchanges. As Norrick (2007) points out, one of the primary reasons for sharing narratives are "opportunities for co-narration and laughing together" (134). Tellability allows other interlocutors or active participants into the narrative because each person is invested in the "news" being shared (29). Each action is news. Agar (2005) provides an example.

> If I tell a story that begins, "The funniest thing happened this morning. I woke up, went into the bathroom, and brushed my teeth," I doubt that any co-tellers within range will be inspired to join in. The story is too much routine to be tellable. On the other hand, if I opened with

"I started to brush my teeth and the toothpaste was full of fire ants," co-tellers would jump into the story with their views as to how and why such a thing could happen." (29)

In the classroom, each student, with a teacher facilitating, can provide a voice in the making and the performance of narratives. Each action created by every student has meaning. When students are the ones making and sharing narratives, they are all invested in its direction as a co-authored process.

Even as a teller works to design a story appropriate to the local audience and context, the audience is already imposing a designing of its own, interrupting, correcting, co-narrating (Agar 2005, 136). From a teaching perspective, what is important "is not a matter of re-telling stories after another person is finished, instead what is important is the reconstruction rather than the simple recall of ordered events" (Norrick 2007, 139). How a story comes together can help students create meaning because they are invested in the construction.

EMBEDDEDNESS

Embeddedness is the third dimension. It refers to "the extent to which a personal narrative is an entity unto itself, separate from prior, concurrent, and subsequent discourse. It is related to turn organization, thematic content, and rhetorical structuring" (Ochs and Capps 2001, 37). How attached or detached the narratives are to other conversations is both contextual and situational. "In every story there exists dialectic between teller and listener and at some horizons and listening fuse . . . and as our lived worlds merge, engagement begets reciprocity and participation in the world of the other and evokes from us the call to act" (Polakow 1985, 827). On the one hand, narrative is simply a performance, detached from other narratives. On the other hand, the surrounding discourse and social activity are important because this can change the way the stories are embedded in other discourses and narratives. In traditional teaching, a teacher provides a form of performance as a narrative is presented. However, when children use stories and play, many other narratives can surface because the students who actually participate in a fictional world are building them. For example, students who use narrative to move into a fictional world as a pirate can reference their narratives while they are in the fictional world. This connects to frame (Goffman 1974). Participants, like the students in the world of pirates, can switch frames, from that of classroom instruction to that of narrative fiction, to those of personal viewing that can include the frames of fictional roles. Students may discuss ways often moving back and forth between the classroom frame and the fictional frame. Many pirate-related stories, for example, can surface and resurface because the narratives are embedded in the fictional world evoked through the telling of stories.

LINEARITY

As the fourth dimension of narrative, linearity is concerned with the narrative's order. With performed narratives, the story is told in recovered chronological order—a closed temporal order. The narrative follows a prescribed order when made and performed. However, at the other end of the continuum, we have open temporal order. An example of this could be brainstorming where narratives are shared after an impulse to share them. When students are playing, they exchange ideas, as they think of them often in a nonlinear fashion. If one examined all the narratives, they would seem entangled, yet this is a "healthy disorder" (Pagnucci 2004). This entanglement consists of various types of narratives in varying degrees that are supported or discarded by other listeners and tellers. From a learning perspective, it is valuable to look at what is said, not said, and how it relates to other narratives especially during the sort of play that students engage in when using the pedagogy of process drama.

MORAL STANCE

Moral stance is the last dimension presented by Ochs and Capps (2001) that refers to narratives' evaluation. They ask, are narratives, open, uncertain, or fluid? Do the narratives postulate moral ethics or code or do they ask the students to consider their own moral wrestlings? "Moral wrestling" is when we are presented with conflicting ideas that go against our natural impulses. We wrestle with ideas of whether the action or choice is right or wrong. When Ochs and Capps (2001) refer to morals, they see them as the "traditional ideas of morality, the nature of the good—the just society, right action, the values one lives by." They see the morals found in narratives occurring as an unraveling process. From a classroom context, I think of the widespread program Character Counts, where students are asked to concentrate on moral values, one per week. For Ochs and Capps (2001), this is too defining; it tells the students how to act. They do not see narratives as tight bundles, but instead gathered from fragments of conversations that can invite moral thinking. It is the reflection and the weighing of ideas that promote moral wrestling.

In this study, I struggle with how these dimensions of narratives affect how students construct meaning. How do I recognize when I as the teacher embed narratives or reduce tellability or tellership? How do I account for this in classroom teaching using process drama and story? Before these questions can be addressed, one must look at the difference between theater and process drama.

The terms "drama" and "theater" are often used interchangeably. I use "theater" to refer not only to the physical space where plays are rehearsed and performed, but also to a study of what it takes to create a play. "Theatre indicates the more formal study of the techniques of acting and stagecraft, often culminating in a performance in front of an audience. Theatre in this sense is primarily concerned with the acquisition of a body of skills and knowledge, in other words learning about the subject" (Taylor and Warner 2006, 31–32).

An actor performs in a play. However, in this context, I refer to "play" as a child's pretending in an imaginary world. However, "at its simplest, drama is wondering, 'What if . . . ?' The term process drama usually distinguishes the particular kind of complex improvised dramatic event . . . [L]ike theater, the primary purpose of process drama is to establish an imagined world, a dramatic 'elsewhere' created by the participants as they discover, articulate, and sustain fictional roles and situations" (O'Neill 1995, xvi). O'Neill (1995) believes process drama relies on improvisation and episodic events to create a drama world: "The episodic structure of process drama allows the gradual articulation of a complex dramatic world and enables it to be extended and elaborated" (xvi). The dramatic "elsewhere" allows students and teachers to move within the drama world.

Because drama experiences occur in fictional worlds when students imagine they are elsewhere, their feelings (which may never be shared) and the movements (which may only be seen as a tilt of the head) connect with and amplify their thoughts of other people, times, and places. According to Wilhelm and Edmiston (1998), drama worlds are suffused with empathy because they "exist in the hearts, voices, and hands of children and their teachers" (5). These worlds are experienced as children and the teacher interact with each other. Narratives are necessary in process drama, since "drama is the act of crossing into the world of story" (Booth 2005, 13).

Heathcote Johnson, and O'Neill (1984) note: "A broad definition of educational drama is 'role-taking,' either to understand a social situation more thoroughly or to experience imaginatively via identification in social situations. Dramatic activity is the direct result of the ability to role-play—to want to know how it feels to be in someone else's shoes" (49).

In the 1960s, Heathcote pioneered process drama where the teacher takes on a role, called "teacher-in-role," entering the fiction to help students question, enact, and engage in the world they have created. Students, too, take on roles entering social situations not as students, but as characters in the imagined world of a story. This work is not concerned with training actors. Heathcote shared how process drama could be used to develop the "humanness" of students while promoting social and emotional development.

DRAMA

I am not concerned with traditional theater, but instead with process drama, which involves children with adults playing in an imaginary world. Producing a play is different than the verb "to play" which includes when a child pretends to be someone else. Unlike theater, process drama requires students to simultaneously engage in pretend play. "In pretend play, people pretend together to move and talk and interact as if they are whatever people or creatures they want to be, in any time or space, engaged in any imagined activity" (Edmiston 2008a, 9). Bolton, Davis, and Lawrence (1986) view an actor's experience as quite different: "Now if we move into theatre, the actors are in a very different order of experiencing, a difference that is crucial. The degree to which the actors can say 'it is happening now; and I am making it happen' is significantly reduced or overshadowed by an orientation towards interpretation, repeatability, projection and sharing with an audience" (165). However, with pretend play and process drama, a child or teen can be anywhere at any time. He or she can play with others who agree to play in an imaginary setting with them.

Practitioners and theorists have used varying terms to describe how they implement drama. There are two main approaches to educational drama, creative drama and drama in education, the main term used in the United Kingdom before the term "process drama" (O'Neill 1995) became more prevalent. "These two approaches rise out of the national traditions in education and in drama, but differ in emphasis and strategies, yet they both are considered art forms and processes of learning" (McCaslin 1996). "In 1972, the term 'creative drama' was introduced by the Children's Theater Association of America to represent an improvisational, process-centered form of drama in which participants are guided by a leader to imagine, enact, and reflect upon the human experience" (Wagner 1998, 10). Creative drama usually starts with warm-ups and exercises for relaxation, with a story at the center of the teaching lesson, but with the teacher on the sidelines of any fictional world. Drama in education, using Heathcote's term, plunged into pretending to be elsewhere. The teacher does not remain on the sidelines but joins in as a full participant in what Heathcote calls "teacher-in-role." Unlike creative drama where the story is simply re-created by techniques such as using pantomime, role-playing, or music, in this work, I examine educational drama where stories are more than a retelling or as a stimulus for a dramatic action. In this work, with process drama and the pedagogy of dramatic inquiry, stories are presented not so students can witness a polished performance, but so they can learn with and from stories.

Students constantly need to adapt to the drama. Davis, Sumara, and Luce-Kapler (2008) stress that when children are engaged in play, they are involved in complex learning. Learning is "a playful phenomenon (that is) about moving into and through an evolving space of possibility" (83). In process drama, students use stories to help them move and not only create possibilities but have a "lived through experience" (Heathcote 1984, 97). The stories constitute an alternative set of possibilities when they provide entry into another world and/or sustain the drama. For Davis, Sumara, and Luce-Kapler (2008), using teaching in a complex manner is not about, "how to control what happens, but how to participate mindfully in the unfolding possibilities" (226).

Process drama, educational drama that Heathcote Johnson, and O'Neill (1984) showed could be used for learning, invites students to co-construct with the teacher as they move into a fictional world as "critical co-investigators" of both any fictional context and its implication for the lives of students and others in the everyday world. Using improvisation, students reflect and can act on their ideas. According to Edmiston (2003), teachers and students are able to reflect from "inside the drama." Reflection inside the drama and reflection in an ordinary discussion differ. In the drama we are not only able to look at the significance of the events and interpret them as "ourselves," but we can also do this from the perspective of the person we are pretending to be. By focusing on inquiry, students engage and explore together what they wish to learn or understand. Edmiston (2010) stresses, "Dramatic inquiry dramatizes inquiries about life and it is improvised when actions and responses in particular social situations within imagined cultural communities are not predetermined but are collaborative created by participants and mediated by adults" (257).

Process drama focuses on discovery and meaning making, not product. It is a systematic way to teach and learn using drama. As Booth (2005) notes, there are many stories in process drama: "In story drama, there is the story we begin with—our shared story; the story of the drama—our created story; and the stories triggered by the drama from student's life experiences—our own life stories. As teachers we work with students as co-constructors of a common story, represented through drama, based on and integrating pieces of the stories we have met and the stories we have lived" (13).

This work will examine deeply the many stories that occur during, and as result of, storymaking and storytelling, with and without the use of drama. Narratives can appear as "messy" stories without ending or simply narrative fragments. In fact, an unfinished story often provides the spark or pretext for process drama (O'Neill 1995).

Narratives are an integral part of creating a drama world. They operate differently in process drama than in regular theatrical drama. In theatrical drama, one story is represented—though we can hear other vantage points through the characters and actions in the play, story is often one controlling narrative. For example, in *A Doll's House*, by Henrik Isben, a story is represented as theater, detailing Nora's struggle in society. We learn about this struggle through her insights and the other characters in the play. The product is an artistic rendering that tells the play's story. In contrast, in process drama, there is no predetermined controlling narrative already written down as a script. Rather, the story or stories are created in process. Bolton (1979) explains that what is important in using drama is what happens between the actual and fictional worlds with the children. This dialectic relationship is where drama comes into play. He goes on to say, "Drama is a metaphor. Its meaning lies not in the actual context nor in the fictitious one, but in the dialectic set up between the two" (128). The teacher facilitates how students construct meaning with the students in both worlds.

I believe that when drama is a group sharing of a dramatic situation, it is more powerful than any other medium in education for achieving our pedagogic aims. But this kind of drama puts tremendous strain and tremendous responsibility on the teacher. He has a very positive role because children left to themselves can only work horizontally at a "what if." Imagination is the psychological process that takes a particular form in dramatic activity. It requires that the participant consciously adopt an "as if mental set, simultaneously holding two worlds in his mind, the present or real world and the absent or fictitious world should happen next" level (Bolton 1979, 44).

Stories can be used to help students engage in both worlds and with stories; students can explore possibilities with the stories that are co-created using process drama.

David Booth (1994) uses the term "story drama" detailing how his approach to process drama combines story and drama in a systematic way for learning:

> In my work, story and drama are forever linked. Even now, when I am reviewing a new picture book or novel for children, I cannot escape the possibilities that flood my drama-structured mind. Similarly, when preparing to work with a group of youngsters for the first time in drama, I cannot imagine entering the room without a range of stories ready to tell or read aloud. Perhaps I require the safety net of narrative in order to attempt to leap into creating stories together through drama. (8)

Much of Booth's work is invaluable for my study, especially the attention he gives to narrative in connection with drama. He values the work of professional storytellers. In *Storyworks* (2000), Booth has written with professional storyteller Bob Barton and provides as an authority the work of the teller and his work as a reading/process drama specialist. Booth takes a text, usually a children's story or young adult book and, using process drama, creates and explores the stories that arise from concentrating on the situations of the characters. However, the story is a pretext; it is the entrance to a drama world where it and the stories behind the stories in the text can also be explored. As a professional storyteller, I am also interested in how told stories in addition to the published stories Booth uses can be used as a pretext with process drama: "In drama in education (DIE) or process drama, classroom practitioners transform texts, sometimes using them as starting points, but always exploring the spaces (i.e., a realistic problem that could be solved) between episodes in a story to create an imagined world and change the story into something quite new" (Wagner 1976, 7).

O'Neill (1995) shares that "a pre-text has a precise function that goes much further than merely suggesting an idea for dramatic exploration" (7). Overall, "the pre-text furnishes an excuse for immediate action or task or carries an implication of further action, so that the participant's anticipation and search for fulfillment can begin" (23). In other words, any story used as a pretext for entry with a drama world, is not a text to be staged, but rather a narrative to be used to generate other narratives as students and teacher imagine together that they are elsewhere.

In theater, the actors, playwright, and director work together to create a play which in performance becomes the product. The play is created as a collaborative outcome of their dramatic interpretations and choices as they turn a script into a performance. Bolton (1992) stresses that a play's success depends upon the actors, whereas, in process drama, success depends on how well students are engaged:

When I first started to teach drama, any occasion when a small group was brought out to the front carried the implication that the "success" of the exercise rested on the "actors" ... In the usage I am now suggesting its success is dependent on the imagination of the "directors," for the "actors" may simply be offering themselves for manipulation, merely carrying out the director's instructions using appropriate "descriptive" technique. (25)

In contrast with staged drama, which is theater with an external audience, process drama has no external audience. According to O'Neill (1995), process drama is an "exploratory dramatic activity where the emphasis in on process rather than product" (xv). The purpose of drama is "to establish an imagined world, a dramatic 'elsewhere' created by the participants as they discover, articulate, and sustain fictional roles and situations" (xvi). Process drama is not intended to be viewed by an outside audience as in theater.

In process drama, children and young adults share their reflections within the fictional world as they make meaning about any imagined events and their accompanying narratives. They do it from the perspective of characters or fictional roles. Children "think from within a dilemma instead of talking about a dilemma" (Wagner, quoting Heathcote, 1976, 127). Drama becomes a reflective tool, so students can wander within both the fictional and classroom worlds. As Wilhelm and Edmiston (1998) observe,

If students are exploring questions through drama they will need to stop "playing" with a question and think about what has been "played." As they interact, the students will be constructing new understandings which may clarify some ideas yet "problematize" others. Our interventions can influence this process when we direct the student's attention toward making or interpreting the fictional world. (88–89)

When students' reflections are formed by inquiry, questions within process drama can be considered "dramatic inquiry."

In the sixties, Heathcote revolutionized educational drama by employing a teacher-in-role within process drama. Wagner (1976) states that "one of Heathcote's most effective teaching ploys is her skillful moving in and out of role. She goes into role to develop and heighten emotion; she comes out of it to achieve distance and the objectivity needed for reflection" (127). The teacher engages students, not as a teacher but as if she is someone else within the fictional world, often a character from a story in story drama. Neelands (1984) shares, "It is . . . important to remember that the purpose of the teacher role is to put the children into the immediate situation where they have to do the thinking, the talking, the responding, the decision making, and the problem solving . . . It's essential . . . to step back and push the group into using their own combined resources as a way of dealing with whatever arises" (50). Thus, the teacher's function in role is not to entertain, and rarely to instruct, but rather to promote students' learning. It is important to stress that when the teacher is in role the power can shift within the relationship—between teacher and students (Heathcote 1984). If a teacher takes on an authoritative role such as a ship captain, he or she can address students according to rank. However, if she becomes a lowly pirate who sweeps up the ship, then the students can address this pirate differently if they are in authority, such as a pirate in charge of guarding prisoners. When power shifts, so does the authority for creating and telling stories. Thus, the teacher can significantly affect what and how students create narratives.

The stories in dramatic inquiry create possibilities for students to co-create narratives, but it is the teacher's role as a critical co-investigator that encourages learning. According to King, (1995) when students are engaged in storymaking, the possibilities are open and many: "The process of storymaking leads us along our inner path, to find the places where stories live. There are many ways to begin and no one way works for everyone every time. What is always required is acceptance—of ourselves and of our stories" (16). Stories can serve as entrance points into the drama. However, in order to co-construct a story, one must accept that each person can actively participate in the storymaking.

Using story as mode of entry and sustained curiosity allows students to both engage and challenge within their inquiries. Possibilities open in this skilled shifting, offering many pathways to follow within the drama. For example, in the England experience, a student was simply playing without direction on the snowmobile—messing around, not involved in the drama. Edmiston asked the child, "What is this for?" The child created a narrative, with the help of Edmiston, that he was checking the snowmobile's speed. Edmiston used this new information to keep the student involved in the drama by asking him to check the speed continuously to let him know when the snowmobile was ready. This teaching move kept the student invested in the drama and subsequently the learning pathways to follow within the drama. With the teacher, as a class, direction is negotiated.

Moffett (1983), in his analysis of drama and narrative as aspects of the "universe of discourse," advocated dramatic improvisation as a powerful way to imaginatively enter the world of story.

> Improvisation can be used as an entrée into a literary work soon to be read: the teacher abstracts key situations—say, Cassius' efforts to persuade Brutus to join the conspiracy—and assigns this as a situation to improvise before students read the work, so that when they do it they already have an understanding of what is happening and how differently the characters might have behaved. This kind of prelude also involves students more with the text. (91)

Similarly, O'Neill (1995) shares that "improvisation is at the heart of the event" (xvi–xvii). Inside a drama world, stories do not look the same as they do when used in organized storytelling. Improvisation that is directed by the teacher can allow for deeper inquiry when the improvisation is structured. The teacher can facilitate students' moves among fictional situations in the drama world as they wonder how their characters might behave in possible scenarios. Plus, the teacher can introduce other characters to test their ideas. Although a script is not used, the teacher does plan strategically but not for how the story will unfold; rather, the teacher plans for deepening inquiry by shifting viewpoints and reflecting to make meaning of the events by mediating the process of creating fictional situations within dramatic inquiry.

Bob Barton and David Booth (1990), like Moffett, regards story drama as a way of accessing and performing the world of an ongoing narrative. In process drama, story is constantly being shaped by the negotiations among students and teacher. As students improvise, they "think in and through the materials of the medium" and "control significant aspects of what is taking place" (O'Neill 1995, 1).

Neelands (1984) notes an overlap between story and drama:

> Although drama is not story, there are interested comparisons between the way "meanings" are constructed in both story and drama. In a sense, the teacher is using role to start "writing" the drama. . . . Because the teacher is trying to work indirectly (i.e., at an affective rather than intellectual level,) the writing is suggested and resonant, offering a number of open-ended possibilities to which the group can respond . . . [T]he difference of course is that drama offers the "readers" the chance to become involved into the action and to share in "writing" of the drama with the teacher. (4)

As Heathcote (1978) shares, the living through experience of process drama as students create imagined events "is not stories the students re-enact; they simply live through some events as best they may be using what they already understand to 'inform' the situation and give them a hold of it. And this, in turn, leads them to need further information, gleaned through the living-through" (65). One way to further information is when adults tell stories. At the same time, the ongoing narrative collaboratively created by participants in process drama is not created the same way as a told story. As Heathcote (1984) notes,

"Any story will be constructed by a different form than that of a narrative because theater is a synchronic art not a diachronic one, stories must be broken into episodes and each episode made to yield the learning experience the teaching requires" (131). When I was teaching using the *Titanic* as the subject of the process drama, I deliberately did not tell all the events of the story of the *Titanic*. Instead, I presented this event in episodes. An example of this would be when a student responded as an engineer. She shared her account of building structures to withstand icebergs. Later, students responded differently in a new role in a different episode when we met Captain John Smith and tried to comfort him at his time of loss. Another time, students prepared to meet the press. Each episode was a way we shared, experienced, told, and contested why the *Titanic* sank. Stories did not always link the episodes. For example, we made a map charting the ship's direction to move our drama into learning about the danger of icebergs and still other devices to move to talking with Captain John Smith. I deliberately changed the setting to be a quiet place, so all ideas could be heard. We could hear Smith as he cried about the loss.

In dramatic inquiry, students' questions not only create an entrance into the drama world, but also open up new narrative possibilities. Edmiston (2009) illustrates:

> In a 9th grade high school urban English classroom students spoke as if on the telephone with their congressional representative, represented by Brian, to begin to explore their inquiry question: what might be done to help refugees in Darfur. Later, they deepened inquires as they shifted perspective to imagine they were journalists, incognito, entering Sudan to document events and make them public. (84)

Co-constructing learning using stories can change teaching. Narratives are used for performance in everyday narratives and provide an understanding of process drama and namely dramatic inquiry, highlighting the importance of seeing narratives and improvisation as tools for learning.

CHAPTER FOUR

UNDERSTANDING STORYTELLING

As a professional storyteller for the past twenty-seven years, I have acquired a unique understanding of the art. I have used storytelling on a daily basis for more than fifteen years in the classroom, designing basic and advanced storytelling classes. I also have created and taught storytelling as it applies to history, reading, English, composition, and other co-curricular subject areas. For nine of those years, I worked in a small, rural school district in California as the first full-time high school storytelling teacher in the country. In these roles, I designed teaching lesson plans using story and guiding students to find meaning of their learning using narratives. It soon became difficult to design a teaching plan without using narrative. As one of my students, Jennifer, shared, "Mr. Cordi, you use story in all your teaching. I have had many classes with you, and I have noticed this." As I began to explain, she stopped me and said, "You don't understand. I just wanted you to know that I liked it, and I know it works." Jennifer was shy in class, and I had no idea how story affected her. I learned to listen to students like Jennifer. Like Campano (2007) recalls, "over the course of my teaching career, my investigation into my students' experiences and my own reflections about the relationship between teaching and research became inextricably linked context of inquiry" (9).

I explore and reflect through formalized methods how story can assist with my story-based teaching to help students make meaning from the use of narrative teaching. By questioning and troubling my story teaching in the form of "story lessons," I can improve my own story teaching practice. Through personal reflection and reflexivity, I gain new understandings of my teaching. In addition to examining my practice of story lessons over the years, I also examine not only my teaching efforts using narrative, but how they are used when working in conjunction with my present understanding of process drama.

For the past five years, I have engaged in doctoral study as a researcher, participant-observer, and student, studying process drama and its connection to teaching and learning. As a storytelling teacher, I reflect upon story connections questioning how process drama and storytelling can work in tandem. In the winter of 2007, in a rural elementary school in England, traveling with my advisor, Brian Edmiston, and process drama teacher, Tim Taylor, for three intense school days, I videotaped, assisted, taught, and observed process drama at work in its form as dramatic inquiry. We worked with thirty-four students ranging in ages from five to nine. During this time, we employed narrative in a dramatic exploration working collaboratively with students to make meaning. We entered a drama world of mountain climbing to assist and save a wounded mountain climber. Drama was used to help students create and engage the narratives.

During school hours, except lunchtime, with our help, students built this drama and explored, in dramatic story-based ways, how to help the injured climber. They created first aid stations and snowmobiles out of oversized wooden blocks, designing their story and play around these representations. These wooden models invited narration from both the students and the teacher. They told the story first and used the models to sustain it. The blocks became places where drama was realized. Both telling and sharing informed this realization. What was critical was the teachers' use of mediation as tools (Vygotsky 1978) to help students make meaning from the dramatic experience. Mediation advanced learning and the unfolding narratives. This mediation, by the teachers often occurred within the narratives. For example, blocks became helicopters flown to assist the rescue and allowed students and adults to communicate within the drama world narratives. Using narrative-based teaching was one way students were invited into the drama and also how the drama was sustained over time (teachers also employ other tools, such as drawing, writing, tableau, and dramatic conventions). As the teachers and students told stories, they created their part of the fictional stories and enacted them.

Environments, story lessons, and process drama can be considered story events because each story event calls for students and teachers to act differently than the other. As Bauman (1978) notes, the events can change the culture. The interactions and expectations of the events are not the same. Story events invite different levels of participation, distinguish different roles of the teacher and students, and assign different ways story can be represented and shared. I will explore the teaching in the story events that can elevate or hinder a student's meaning making by writing about these experiences from a personal perspective. I write about how the cultural context changes with the events. One way to record and reflect upon this is to employ ethnography as a research method.

Academics often write from an impersonal nature when reporting research. Schubert (1991) notes that teachers "become akin to participants on assembly lines rather than professionals who conceptualize, act, and reflect on work derived from deep commitment" (210). Jungck (2001) adds that "the dominant perception of what is considered 'real' or legitimate research has functioned to artificially separate teachers from researchers, teaching from researching, and theorizing from practicing" (333). In traditional research methods, the researcher's role is often marred or impersonal. An impersonal voice would not work since the subject of the research is my voice—my story teaching practices and how I can improve them. My voice supports this study. Richardson (1997) questions, as do I, "why we don't include 'I' in our research." She continues, "Academics are given the story-line that 'I' should be suppressed in their writing, that they should accept homogenization and adopt the all-knowing, all-powerful voice of the academy, but contemporary philosophical thought raises problems that exceed and undermine the academic story line. We are always present in our texts, no matter how we try to suppress ourselves" (3). However, as Campano (2007) laments, "some university-based researchers may disregard the stories of teachers because they are not rigorous, are too subjective, cannot be generalized, are self-absorbed, and so on." He continues, "Why engage in the risky. Why tell stories from and about the classroom?" (17). For me, the answer is simple; sharing my story and teaching practices is an effective way to address my work in the classroom. As writer Campano (2007) makes clear, students (and teachers) write not only from experience but for experience; storytelling becomes an ongoing process of inquiry and discovers that is potentially generative (18).

As teacher and researcher, I depend upon experience and the ability to rethink or "bend back" (Guralnik 1982, 45). By these experiences as a storytelling teacher, I am a "teacher-as-reflector" (Schön, 1983) writing about my own practice. As a reflexive researcher/teacher, my analysis is my own, a "custom job" (Nightingale 1999, 228). "Reflexivity then, urges us to explore the ways in which a researcher's involvement with a particular study's influence acts upon and informs such research" (Nightingale and Cromby 1999, 228). Reflexivity places me within the research. According to Scott and Morrison (2007), reflexivity may be "defined as the process by which a researcher comes to understand how they are positioned in relation to the knowledge they are producing, and indeed, is an essential part of that knowledge-producing activity" (201). Positioning is key.

In my research, I must be cognizant of how I position students when using story lessons and how I am positioned by storytelling events and the formed culture that results from the storytelling events. I also must see how students are positioned not only from story, but also from using narrative in conjunction with process drama. I serve many positions in this work as a student learning from the experience, a teacher instructing students, a teacher engaged in drama with students, and a teacher designing instruction. In all cases, I reflect upon and analyze these positions. Although I employ many roles, all data is filtered through my understanding. I interpret how the data are gathered, processed, and organized. What is also important is how the idea of self helps the narration of my research (Lichtman 2006, 12). Self is integral to my study. In order to talk about self, I must be able to narrate self.

> The construction of selfhood, it seems, cannot proceed without a capacity to narrate. Once we are equipped with that capacity, we can produce a selfhood that joins with others, that permits us to hark back selectively to our past while shaping ourselves for the possibilities of an imagined future . . . [O]ur stories also impose a structure, a compelling reality on what we experience, even a philosophical stance . . . Storymaking is the medium for coming to terms with the surprises and oddities of the human condition and for coming to terms with our imperfect grasp of that condition. (Bruner 2002, 86)

The storyteller/researcher interprets the data, becoming a filter for understanding, and shapes the information through meaning making (Bruner 2002). Researchers who choose to write using methods such as autoethnography must be good tale-tellers. This is because the subject is their own reflections, and they are often delivered in narrative. However, the lens the researchers uses is a critical one, one that does not often tell the dominant narrative, but instead asks to look for other stories about the subject. The narratives must be told to be experienced, but the writer is the filter for the how the story is perceived. This is why researchers need to be effective narrative tellers. An effective story moves a reader to want more of the account.

Reflective and honest writing requires me to challenge my assumptions. I am doing more than telling a story; instead, I am struggling to understand the imbalance and balance of how my use of stories connected or did not connect to who I am. An example is the difference being raised with Appalachian tradition has to my other identities. My Appalachian identity was one narrative that could compete with my performance identity and my teaching identity. In this study, I examine how they both flow and block each other. Each narrative works within a backdrop of the other narratives. Each identity has assumptions: a person from Appalachia must reside in Appalachia; a person never breaks to explain a story when he is a professional storyteller. As a teacher, however, I need to break a story in order to share a new form of storymaking, namely, process drama. In the classroom, I troubled my assumptions. During my fifteen years of teaching using narratives, I have found myself teaching students from my performance understanding of storytelling. When narrative works in conjunction with process drama, performance is not the outcome, and therefore the basic assumptions of using narrative teaching changes. This methodology allows me to test, evaluate, and frame my thinking concerning both teaching pedagogies. Teachers often do not make time to critically examine their classroom practices. Indeed, in the fifteen years I have taught high school, I have rarely had time to write down my thoughts or evaluate them through a narrative lens. I have tried to make the time, and I did write about my practices, but not in a concerted effort. The ability to reflect is one that must be learned: "The increasing demands on teachers . . . require that they spend more and more time trying to get things done rather than thinking about what they have done or what they will do. Reflection is a luxury most teachers do not have the opportunity to indulge in" (Ladson-Billings 2001, 21). Using narrative in my writing allows me, as a researcher, to attain new information.

I, as the researcher, can only see this work from my understanding. "At every point in our research—in our observing, our interpreting, our reporting, and everything else we do as researchers—we inject a host of assumptions" (Crotty 1998, 17). The social context of the people I am working with will be at the forefront of my analysis.

As Pagnucci (2004) recounts, "in a narrative world there is no such thing as fixed truth. Stories are always fluid, moving, changing. There are no truths, in a narrative life, only different ways to tell the story" (52). "Truth" changes as different contexts are presented.

Because a narrator tells us what happened, where and when, he or she tends to convey an aura of truth along with the narrated events. Indeed, they are the truth from the teller's vantage point at a particular time of the inquiry. Yet that truth may change as the inquiry progresses in a retelling of a story, especially if various actors are consulted (Clandinin and Connelly, 2000).

Stories are meaningful when placed in context. Josselson (2006) adds, "The challenge that confronts us is how to assimilate narrative understanding at a conceptual level in a way that does not return to a modernist frame, but rather to treat them as situated interpretations" (6). As was noted, storytelling events are situational and will be interpreted through a cultural understanding. Another area to avoid is what Clandinin (2000) calls the "Hollywood Plot," where everything neatly works out in the end. When this occurs, "the researcher must make a series of judgments about how to balance the smoothing contained in the plot with what is obscured in the smoothing. To acknowledge narrative smoothing is to open another door for the reader" (181). My teaching does not always end with "happily ever after." In fact, narrative can help extend the traditional ending of a story. Using narratives in teaching can also expand the learning. In this work, I am not concerned with smoothing out my teaching, but instead placing the work under a reflective and reflexive lens.

CHAPTER FIVE

USING STORYTELLING AND STORYMAKING IN MY CLASSES

In this chapter, I examine my work as a teacher and storyteller because the method calls for me not to simply retell my story, but instead to wrestle with the worlds where I was placed in order to dig deeper beyond the surface of my teaching and to position my writing through many lenses.

I need not retell my teaching career, but instead trouble my thinking over significant times in my teaching, including addressing my life before I was a teacher. I explore three elements: stories about my past leading to my first experience as a storyteller; reflections about those stories; and perceptions of storytelling and story used for teaching and creating spaces for student voices.

In the stories about my past and my first experience as a storyteller, I outline how I became a storyteller and how growing up in a storytelling, Appalachian culture directly influences my work as both a professional storyteller and a teacher. I then discuss how perceptions of storytelling and storymaking are used for teaching. I detail and critically review how stories are seen as teaching tools, especially the work of Ruth Sawyer. I also sharply contrast this with my own discoveries using story to teach. Last, I detail how I create a space for student voices by honoring their insight and stories in the classroom and by forming a storytelling club.

When examining these elements, many questions arise, such as the following: How has my personal orientation raised by Appalachian parents influenced my work as a storytelling teacher? How have I taught in both worlds of storytelling and education? How have traditional rules of storytelling affected my risk taking when teaching using story? How important is performance to storytelling? How does improvisation help teaching? Which did I value more—storymaking or storytelling? Do I need to choose one over another? How have and will these choices affect my teaching? I address these questions through critical reflective writing.

My writing depends upon self-reflection. This chapter is deliberately designed to interweave the personal, scholarly, experiential, and professional. I have purposefully avoided presenting some of the material simply as data and some as commentary. With this style of writing, I argue it is all data, and at the same time, it is also all-reflective. All of the information is about my experience through my lens. It is my data, but it is also my bending back to understand more of what has occurred and how it can prepare me to become a better educator using stories. Clearly, story can be both data and written as commentary. I do not separate these categories, but, instead, I deliberately blur the genres.

In order to push myself to understand, I need to release ways I have traditionally accepted when using story and storytelling to teach. In this work, I am trying to let go of what I have learned and know about the world of storytelling and education, so I can gain new understandings of how these worlds both contradict and complement each other. In so doing, I intend to establish what is referred to as a "new middle" (Mora 1993), a cross among story, storytelling, and education. Reflective writing depends on my understanding formed by the social groups I have been in, the ones I was admitted to, and those I had to work to join. This work is about the wrestling to be understood in the worlds of teaching, telling, and something in between.

In this chapter, I resist doing what comes naturally to me—telling the story up front. It is a natural inclination to tell my teaching story as one long autobiography, but in my writing, I share a critical reflection that helps me examine my teaching to improve it. I am not working to perform, so the audience, in this case, the reader, and I share a story with a happy ending. Instead, I am sharing a critical reflection embedded with my narratives and my students in order to understand what has occurred and my place in it. This is more than a collection of stories; instead, it is stories that serve as data so that I can examine the meaning in them. The stories are not tightly woven, but instead deliberately messy. Instead of compact tellable stories, I share stories in an ongoing dialogue. I argue a story has multiple unfoldings, some beginnings, some endings, and still some unresolved pieces. This is the reflection within this chapter. However, to provide a clue, because after all, a particular perspective drives my narrative, it is a story about reexamining what I knew initially about storytelling and using that insight to construct pedagogy. Teaching calls for a different method, suspending what I knew about professional storytelling to accommodate better teaching. This narrative is, in part, about the blocks and intersections guiding this journey. Along the way, I offer comments about testing traditional ways of story use and breaking the rules of storytelling, redesigning story to elevate my teaching, creating story spaces for student stories, and the importance of community over performance. To discuss these practices, I detail classroom examples through thick, narrative stories to engage in critical reflection. As a narrative teacher, I believe these stories will help orient the direction of my writing.

In essence, the narrative teacher believes in the power of story, and so stories become a central tool for teaching and learning. Living the narrative life means rethinking one's whole approach to knowledge. Rather than always pursuing knowledge through analysis and critical thinking that rely on critiquing and dissecting ideas, one seeks narrative. Believers seek to create knowledge through the telling of stories. (Pagnucci 2004, 47)

In writing and reflection on these thick narratives, I can dig deeper into my teaching history to determine how my choices helped inform my pedagogical philosophy and methodology. This narrative must be shared using qualitative measures.

Bochner (2001) argues for qualitative research employing narrative:

> The narrative turn moves from a singular, monolithic conception of social science toward a pluralism that promotes multiple forms of representation and research: away from facts and toward meanings; away from master narratives and toward local stories: away from idolizing categorical thought and abstracted theory and toward embracing the value of irony, emotionality, and activism; away from assuming the stance of disinterested spectator and toward assuming the posture of a feeling, embodied, and vulnerable observer; away from writing essays and toward telling stories. (134–35)

Dewey (1933) describes reflection within the classroom as, "active, persistent, and careful consideration of any belief or supposed form of knowledge in light of the grounds that support it and the further consequences to which it leads" (9). Self-reflection, especially in print, creates a certain messiness, uneasiness, and definite vulnerability (Denzin 2003, 9). However, it is only through this sifting and shifting of experience and analysis where new connections and learning begin. I need to give myself permission to be messy in order to understand how narratives used for teaching can become clearer to me in my teaching practice. Pagnucci (2004) calls this "the pleasure of messiness" and says that "narratives can address contradiction, confusion, and complexity without offering any concrete answers, which is, upon consideration, exactly what real life does" (52). He goes on to say that "living the narrative life is about figuring out what counts" (54). In this chapter, I wrestle with "what counts" in retelling and refocusing my teaching life as a storytelling teacher. I open doors, not only to my classroom, but also to my actions within the classroom, hoping to learn from my promising teaching practices as well as my mistakes. I will not censor my actions, but instead detail them for understanding. In some cases, this analysis will invite change. To discuss these practices, I detail classroom examples through thick, narrative stories to engage in critical reflection. As a narrative teacher, I believe these stories will help me orient the direction of my writing.

As Kemmis (1985) underscores, reflection is a personal and social process. It is personal because I draw upon my perspectives and insights in my teaching. As I reflect, I reference my work in the form of dialogue. It is social because the dialogue is not confined to the voices I have to offer but incorporates many other voices to help further my understanding. This includes my parents, other teachers, and my students. I have to admit, in order to write about these subjects, I needed to change how I felt about my work separating my inhibitions of how telling "your story" can be seen through an academic lens. For years, I have known the value of telling stories, but when using my own experiences as a model for reflection, I had to remind myself of narrative's ability to address and revisit the past to inform the present. However, the world of academe is only beginning to concern itself with the world of the storyteller. In my coursework, outside of folklore and storytelling classes, I rarely found storytelling as an oral art emphasized; instead there was a heavy emphasis on narrative as a written work. In fact, in general, professional storytelling is new and often seen as indifferent by the academy. In turn, storytellers don't attend too much to storytelling as a study beyond performance. Storytellers generally don't study the work but instead work on how to improve their own storytelling performances. There are exceptions for both, but generally, the two have not embraced each other. I knew this before I engaged in this study, using my writing to merge these worlds. I hoped to sustain the voice of a storyteller, but also keep a voice that could be recognized for academe claim. Few professional storytellers have written academe work, but I felt a need to not separate my voice as a storyteller, but to merge and apply it to my understanding of scholarship. In contrast, narrative is recognized in scholarship.

As outlined in chapter 3, Campano (2007) shares how narrative can be used to understand the relationship between research and teaching. Writing stories can bring out perspectives. As Geertz (1973) supports, story is a process of construction, and by working with stories, a "battery of interpretations" (3) can assist the researcher to think about the past, present, and possible. Using methods like autoethnography creates an engagement between self and the social contexts—in this case, the world of teaching and the world of the academe. In this work, I examine and contest the social world of professional storytelling with the classroom. Professional storytellers are generally not credentialed teachers. Instead, they are guest artists. However, since I served both as a credentialed teacher and a professional storyteller, I had a different access to my students and the schools. I could work with story beyond one performance or a week in residence. Instead, I needed to look at longer and even stronger applications of story and story use in the classroom. I also had the invitation to refer back using story work in additional lessons. Saying all this, I also was the storyteller who came in and developed a program of stories for entertainment or to teach about one issue, such as antibullying or a time in history such as the Civil War, and could measure my work as a storytelling teacher in a continual classroom against being the guest teller in another teacher's class. In this study, I examine these worlds and demonstrate how I was confused as to which way I was to use story in my classroom because of my experience as a guest teller.

As a teacher, I not only listen to my voice, but I also recall and focus on my students' voices. I am able to engage, look back on my story use, and see how my students and I were restricted by my teaching and also how we advanced because of it. Addressing these worlds can create a tension that can help me understand my role in both academic and storytelling environments. In writing, I needed not to worry how my work might fit within an academic tone, but instead, concentrate on how I had taught. Using writing that incorporates my own narratives allows me to dialogue, and in that communication, many voices can help my search in improving my teaching. This method helps me make sense of my teaching life. As I write and reflect, I can revisit my students or even my own practice. As Labov (1972) notes, in telling the story, I can bring past action to the forefront. My students' stories take priority if I make it the point of reflection. I use this to align my thinking. I can in a real sense speak and hear the voices of other teachers and students as I recall their narratives along with my own. In a story where I find a journal from a homeless student who lived on our school's roof, I incorporate these stories that my students ask in telling about the experience. In my writing, I can reexperience this event in order to understand it.

> Once we understand that communication embodies both the personal and the cultural, and then we legitimate the need to show how individuals use communication personally to cope with difficult moments in their lives. This brings up intricate connections among experiences, grasp what personal experiences mean, and express those meanings to one's self as well to others. (Bochner 2001, 12)

Attempting to be honest about my beginnings as a storyteller and teacher as well as my developments over the years, I needed to allow the narratives to speak so I could understand them. This reflection is about being in both worlds where in each world I have a different voice. Let us examine the worlds in which I write. First, I need to acknowledge there are other worlds in my teaching that I do not extend. This is the world of a white, married man. I recognize this position of viewing the world also invites and deters other perspectives. In California, I taught many migrant workers' children. I would never state I understand or could relate my world to their work in the fields. In this work, I discuss my world of being a story listener, hearing my students' stories of working in the fields. This was my first understanding of the educational use of story. I then dismiss the world of the professional storyteller where I learned the rules of storytelling and mix these worlds with my world as a high school educator, process drama teacher, and PhD student and college professor. From this intermingling, I consider how all these worlds inform my writing. Clearly, this methodology supports the process. As I engage in dialogue, I allow my stories and reflections to describe and speak to my history. As I steer away from answering as only an academic," but instead being multivoiced, I believe I become more diverse in my academic analysis. I learn that my choices are dependent on whom I am speaking to and how I am speaking. As my voice is more personal, I can speak from an academic context when needed. I can speak as a storyteller and storymaker as needed. There is room for personal narratives along with academic awareness. However, my personal reflection is never gone from my many voices as a teacher, teller, and university professor. As I reflect, I see this as a blending of voices which includes my academic training and practice, but when my voice as a storyteller needs to surface, I can choose that as well to teach my students. As Becker (2007) adds,

> Academics favor a few classic personae whose traits color academic prose, shape academic arguments, and make the resulting writing more or less persuasive to various audiences. Those personae inhabit a world of scholars, researchers, and intellectuals in which it is useful or comfortable to be one another of these people. The academic-intellectual world has an ambiguous and uneasy relation to the ordinary world, and many academics worry about their own relation to ordinary people. (33)

My narrative has helped form the foundation I have used as a storytelling teacher. In many ways, I am my own first audience. I want to understand my work but also include other readers who are interested in my reflection as scholarship. My writing will include my stories as my method of inquiry. However, the standard "boring" writing where the points are "organized and outlined" may "undercut writing as a dynamic creative process." Instead, my writing will reflect a narrative understanding and not the "homogenized voice of science." Instead, I engage in "narratives that situate one's own writing in other parts of one's life such as disciplinary constraints, academic debates, departmental politics, social movements, community structures, research interests, familial ties, and personal history. They offer critical reflexivity about the writing self in different contexts" (Richardson 1997, 474). In this case, I situate myself, and my writing, within the classroom. However, before I can look at this, I must explore my work within a professional storytelling context before I became a storytelling teacher.

I balance how much of my story I share and review. I constantly wonder what I should leave out and keep in the narrative. Where do I start? How has story become part of what I do? I have carefully selected each story to help address my teaching practices. Each story helps to inform what I understood in the past with story and storytelling to inform my current understanding. Each story is a window to my understanding and questions. Many stories began in my childhood.

My parents are from West Virginia and would often regale all six of us children with tales of rural Appalachia as our teaching lessons. We were reared on traditional or backporch storytelling. It was not performed as a storytelling event, but instead occurred when my parents wanted to entertain or teach us a lesson. Almost daily, my mother, or sometimes my father, would share stories not only about living in West Virginia, but how to live our lives. This goes beyond simply teaching a moral, because my mother used personal stories of family and friends we knew to help inform our own actions. She would tell the story of someone we knew and the wrong choices they made, and in the story, warned us not to make the same choice.

While my mother was preparing dinner, feeding the dog and cats, driving to pick up my father from Goodyear, or taking advantage of the time in between these obligations, she would tell stories. I vividly remember she skillfully wove stories with epigrams such as, "Never take the hat off of someone from West Virginia, you need to be ready for a fight," "Your handshake is as good as your word," or "People who work hard don't have to show it." She would often sing a story about "getting a little dirt on your hands" and ask me, "What kind of dirt were they talking about?" Before I could answer, she would tell me the story of the song where a son's mother tells him to "get a little dirt on your hands, son," and he robs a bank. Mother would laugh because the subject was dirt on the hands and not the type of dirt that comes from committing a crime. When recalling these stories, especially the last one, I begin to sense why story is invaluable for me. My mother would not ask questions like, "What is the lesson?" but instead let the story speak. However, she would tell it to me repeatedly to make sure I understood it. It was different each time—never memorized word for word—instead, designed for my learning and me.

I remember long drives to Goodyear, where my mother would share her childhood struggles, evoking my empathy. In her family, only she and another sibling graduated from high school. My mother spent her days caring for her many siblings living in rural, rustic conditions with no indoor toilets, using water from the spring, and canning for future meals. In looking back at this time, I am sure it affected the way I see how stories are used. She made them personal, and from the beginning, I felt connected to the stories she told. They were the basis of my own learning; in growing up, my mother was the teacher using personal narratives to help me understand the consequences of my decisions. If I were complaining, she would share in a nonjudgmental way a story about how far she had walked to school. I remember when my sister Melinda was lying, my mother told about how she lied to her father, and although he never said a word about it, he knew. She had to build trust up from there. Perhaps this was why I was attracted to professional storytelling in the first place? I come from a culture of story, a place of story, and I have worked hard for the last fourteen years as a teacher and six years as a university professor to help find a place and culture for students' stories. In fact, I feel someone is lost if he or she is not able to tell stories.

In sharing this story, I still wrestle with whether to include this. How important is my personal upbringing? Although I value and realize the importance of being in a storytelling family, how much can it help me understand why I became a storytelling teacher? I need to keep in mind reflective writing is about overlapping narratives and would be considered a blurred genre. In other words, the stories can teach us history, model how to live, be told in song, and serve as a record of events and/or people. A story can contain more than one genre and/or purpose. The story about lying spoke to how trust was inherent as a marker in the culture, but it also was a marker of how to live, suggesting a moral pathway. A storyteller can craft the impact of the stories and for what purpose they are told. Why not include family tradition, especially when it connects to using story to teach? After all, my parents were my first storytellers and also my first teachers. They also shaped the way stories were used in my life—to teach. Just like Jack told about his journeys to anyone who asked or Jack's mother shared the ways of the world by telling Jack stories that turn out to be advice on how to make a decision, stories also raised me.

I am drawn to narrative as a primary classroom tool. I know this began through my mother's circle of understanding, and now from writing this, I realize I have incorporated her teaching practices into my own. Who am I not to value my parents' stories? At the same time, in the context of academia, I have learned I could or even should or might be expected to devalue these stories. In my educational coursework, and in class discussions, we rarely discuss the importance of our backgrounds. We talk about social justice issues and their effects in teaching, but from a distance. We are asked to consider the implications of our roots and place in society, but how often do we tell about it? How often do we share where we are from in direct discussion of our teaching?

Some see these stories, that sometime take the appearance of folktales, although they are real accounts, as a way to escape from the world, but I agree with Mattson and Tatar (2016) that they are more than that; personal tales serve in the same way that they see fairytales:

> Fairy tales and fantasy literature have often been positioned as escapist. But they are less a way out than a way in, an escape into perils and possibilities. Moving in the optative mode, they tell us how things might be, should be, or ought to be.
>
> These stories give us the great "what ifs" and they introduce students to hypotheticals, giving them worlds that may be real yet also characters who shape their identities in much the same way people do in real life. (23)

The tales that we hear around the campfire or on an old couch or inside the classroom say something about the choices we make. However, the teller also tells the story for a reason. After all, my Aunt Ruby used six cups of sugar to make homemade fudge for me for a reason, and that reason is not because she wanted to make fudge. Jack tried to seal up the northwest wind for more reasons than that he was cold. When Jack's mama says, in Ray Hicks' northwest story, "No, Jack, you're just a boy and too young to go out on your own . . . I'll let you go out on your own soon enough" (Smith 2000, 8), she was teaching Jack when to be ready. Linda Williamson (2011), wife of Duncan, the famous Jack teller, states, quoting her husband, "Jack was not one particular person, but a piece of everyman" (9). She continues to share the value of hearing Jack stories. Just like when my mother tells her stories, there is much to figure out. How exactly did Uncle Pete burn down the house? What did he do in the war? Why didn't you have a TV, and Did Aunt Bertha really shoot a cow in the dark of the night? At first sharing about the value of using stories in and out of the classroom can simply be a story, but upon reflection, each time I write about it, I find a little more to be discovered. Like Williamson says of Jack tales, "The storyteller tells us to look to the stories for the answers. The tales about Jack go back a long, long time . . . [M]uch is left to the imagination of the listener; everything is not laid out like in a children's schoolbook. Like dreams, it's always been a mystery (10).

Whether I am hearing a tale about a young boy climbing down from a bean tree or of a young woman who "had to leave the hills to know what she lost," each tale is significant. It is interwoven into a larger story. As I learn to listen to these stories, they help me understand the complex title of being a storyteller.

In my college storytelling class at Ohio Dominican University, I asked my students to study the Jack tales and create their own. I asked them to "honor the traits of a Jack tale," which includes honoring the importance of seeking wisdom and finding helpers on the journey to see their fortune.

Ashley begins her story: "This here is another tale of Jack. We all know about how much Jack ain't too fond of workin.' Jack in his first, honest to goodness, real job. He is as fresh out of college as the milk out of the cow. Jack said he was a movin' to the big city to find him a real, geunwine job."

Tales similar to this one led the class to have real conversations about why Jack might not like working but ends up doing real work that matters. We talked about how Appalachia is often lampooned without knowing the value of the culture and place. I used folktales to help teach about not only Jack, but what Jack represents. We discussed the whys more than the whats that are involved in the Jack tales that are available. A student studying psychology said, "I made my Jack tale stand out by using important morals and values and using symbols to signify their importance . . . [T]his made the story more meaningful." Even though I did provide direct teaching on respecting the roots of Appalachia, beyond providing Jack tales as models, students seriously made this part of each tale. As Pavesic

(2005) states, "Like other art forms, a Jack Tale reflects the society that creates it" (2).

Another world I have engaged in outside of my family that has contributed to my understanding of story and storytelling is the professional storytelling world. In my attempts to make clear how my life story interrelates to my teaching story, in this work, I am trying to let go of what I have come to know about the world of storytelling and education, so I can gain a new understanding of how these worlds contradict and complement each other. It is easy to share my life story. However, it becomes critical writing when these events become significant. As I began to tell my own stories, I changed. Writing about this with a critical lens allows me to "resee" it. There is a social significance and emotional appeal to storytelling. In academia, we are often asked to suspend affect. However, based upon my social contexts, one must take on particular affects in academics as well. For example, to be a teacher, you must be an authority. I am interested in exploring how people, especially students and I, cross outside the lines of any particular world and then recognize our multiple positions. In creating this chapter, I allow this approach to guide my thinking.

My first understanding of storytelling was to entertain. This mindset affected how I saw story in community and educational contexts. I soon stumbled upon stories in professional storytelling that were unlike the traditional home stories my mother and father told whenever and wherever they could. There is a renaissance occurring in storytelling. According to Regina Ress (2007), "The rise in popularity of storytelling itself began in the 1970s . . . The National Storytelling Festival brought together tellers and listeners. The organization that grew around it provided a center for the movement, networking opportunities, and inspiration for the formation of other organizations across the country which sponsored concerts, other festivals and conferences" (1). The site of the International Storytelling Center website (www.storycenter .org) states:

The world's storytelling renaissance began in Jonesborough, a tiny town in the mountains of Tennessee over 40 years ago. On a warm October day in 1973, the town of Jonesborough played host to the first National Storytelling Festival. The festival was small, but something happened that October weekend that has changed forever our culture, this traditional art form, and this Tennessee town.

Now in its 43rd year, the National Storytelling Festival was created by Jimmy Neil Smith, a former journalism teacher and mayor of Jonesborough. His inspiration, quite simply, was a well-told tale heard over a car radio—a story told by Grand Ole Opry star Jerry Clower about hunting in Mississippi. Why not a storytelling festival? Smith wondered.

The first National Storytelling Festival, the first of its kind anywhere in the world, ignited a renaissance of storytelling that is, even today, far-reaching. People across America and the world are rediscovering the simplicity and basic truth of a well-told story.

Ancient storytelling traditions are being recognized and reborn. Storytelling organizations, festivals, and educational events now dot the globe, and the professional storyteller, a fixture in more primitive times and cultures, has reappeared.

Sobol (1999) in his book The Storyteller's Journey: An American Revival, states,

> Much as "The Folksinger" did in the early sixties, "The Storyteller" has developed a certain mythic resonance in popular culture and language—perhaps more in the way of poetic conceit than in an anthropological specific role. Yet it depends for its emotive force on the idea that somewhere, sometime, there is, or was, such a role—a role with expression, didactic, oracular, and community-building functions . . . The storytelling revival has developed its own kind of psychic geography over the years—. (3)

He credits the National Storytelling Festival as a reason for this revival, stating, "The founding of the first storytelling festival in 1973 provided a touchstone for a widespread awakening of cultural missionary spirit" (4). However, that stone had not reached me. That is until in 1987. While attending Kent State University, I had not heard of the renaissance or even a professional storyteller.

At Kent State University, I studied communications as an education major with a focus on journalism education. During the summer of 1987, as a roving journalist searching for stories, I stumbled upon a flyer entitled "Once Upon a Time Storytelling Conference." I called education professor Olga Nelson and asked if I could write a story on the conference, and she agreed. Initially, I was there to cover the event as a news story, not to be personally involved. I had expected a short visit, but the event sparked my interest. The conference consisted of around seventy "old" (at nineteen, I thought anyone over thirty was old) people paying more than $300.00 for a week of stories and workshops about the process. Few smiled, some played with their pencils, but dispositions soon changed after the first storyteller, Bat Burns from Ireland, sang his first story, mesmerizing his audience with his humor. His other selections were both funny and downright sad. He took a popular bank credit card "a unicard" and made a story song from it. He crafted his story with skill that made the story alive when he told it. I was hooked. I no longer wanted to report the story—I wanted to tell it. There was something in the presentation of these stories that in some way mirrored my mother's recounting, although more "rehearsed." His tone, his physical composition, and his style of telling were prepared. When my mother shared, my role was as a listener. I, or my brothers and sisters, were the only audience. In this professional setting, the stories were skillfully designed for a number of audience members. This helped accentuate word choices and delivery. The audience helped to direct the stories. Although my mother had a dynamic and charismatic way of telling, Burns was more focused in his presentation. In some ways, this made us listen more. Until this time, I had never seen a story performed. I pleaded with my editor to allow me more time to write the story. I was hooked; I needed to find out more about storytelling. I stayed the entire week, but it was not enough. I was determined to study this art form to find my own storytelling voice. However, the next step in making this happen did not occur quickly.

In writing this chapter, I wondered if I should include the emotional impact that hearing the professional storytellers had on me. I could have simply stated I first became interested in storytelling the first time I saw a professional storyteller. However, this writing is about creating an emotional experience (Bochner 2001; Ellis 1995, 1997; Jago 2002, 2001). In fact, if professional storytelling did not affect me emotionally then and the way it does now, I would not have explored the teaching that surfaced from storytelling. It was this drive to know more that made me search to be what I witnessed. For example, when I heard Jay O'Callahan tell a sixty-minute story from the point of view of a grandmother of a family who worked in a steel mine in Bethlehem, Pennsylvania, I was in the mine with her. O'Callahan accentuated with his voice and body the woman's pain when her husband was injured from the heat of the iron. When O'Callahan represented this person, he did not tell it as though it happened to her, it happened as she told it. Although he was male, he told the hardship story in first person. He shared his interviews, the people of the story, and adapted the tellable story from these conversations. It was as if the woman were in the room and addressing all of us. In fact, she was. O'Callahan slipped away, and my mind wandered to a wise mother of a steel worker in Bethlehem, Pennsylvania.

Another storyteller, Tim Tingle, author of *Crossing Bok Chitto*, spoke of a young Choctaw girl who leads a runaway slave family to safety. I could tell Tim was there when he told it. He did not remove himself from the experience, but delicately took us on his journey. Tingle transitioned his story to include the spiritual world connection of the Choctaw. Using only words and movement, I felt as though I, too, had entered the spiritual world to help them make this famous crossing. This was quite different than O'Callahan, but in his way, making storytelling a personal art, we still were able to enter the story by his telling.

My friend and colleague Pat Mendoza, who is a Vietnam veteran, shared how the first Vietnam War memorial was named Angelfire. As he shared his stories, he carried me to Vietnam and the emotional spaces there. I had seen theater productions, but always felt I was an observer; however, with the storytellers, I was emotionally attached. It was as though the storytellers through their stories said, "Come sit for a tale and let it take you to this place."

When I listened to the story of my student Angel, of her need to cut herself, I soon realized the school administrators did not want to hear her story. In fact, they were telling her to leave school. Her story was a hard one. When these expectations from the school restricted her voice, I created a place to share where we could all value the listening process, suspend judgment, and lend support. At that time, my role as her teacher was not as important as my role as her storyteller and story listener. She needed to tell this story, even if the school did not hear it. When she told it, my role was to listen and help her accentuate the story. I supported her choice to tell it to an audience of her peers. I worked with her, so she could deliver and perform it. Saying this, there were times when I should have not restricted a tale or two; instead, I listened to the nagging voice of the school saying hardship is not for the public. When I taught at-risk students, who were self-contained because they were not to be trusted with other students (or at least that is how the administration said it), I provided literature for them that was displaced. Their experiences with many authority figures were explaining their action to reduce or escape punishment. I closed off some stories because they swore when telling them, but I finally realized that the stories in their lives consisted of hardship and often they needed to swear when telling the story, to take ownership in telling it. I suspended judgment and perhaps for the first time for many of the students let their world mix with the world of school. I felt after I reduced times to filter their stories, we could learn more about who we were, and why I could teach them. I worked with the student board of our storytelling club to show them how to accept everyone who came to the meetings.

I was not trained to listen this way as a teacher. It was emotional for me to validate the importance of listening within my students' life history as well as my own. It was also emotional to realize how important community was for my students, so I began to build my curriculum with story to create community. When writing about events such as these, I do not hide my feelings for my choices. This deliberate inclusion, I believe, helps to make my stories more authentic and revealing. Everyone has a story to tell, even if it is a difficult one. I began to reexamine how often we allow students to tell their stories. I began to align my own teaching to include more encouragement such as asking, "What do you think of . . . ?" and "What is your insight about . . . ?" After all, as a student, how connected can you be to learning if you feel disconnected to what you are to learn? As teachers, we have students like Angel, who needs to feel wanted before she can learn.

For one year, I found worn out library tape recordings featuring storytellers as my only source for professional storytellers, but these included nationally known Donald Davis, Elizabeth Ellis, and the Folktellers. I mirrored their voices and sounds, trying to imagine how they might physically tell stories. Donald Davis mirrored the style of my mother telling personal Appalachian tales. However, his tales were carefully crafted, so each word was significant. If he repeated something, it was meant to be repeated. Elizabeth Ellis also told personal tales, as well as fairy tales with a feminist slant. It was from her that I learned the power of perspective. Her female characters did not exhibit mousy dispositions but, instead, were powerful.

The Folktellers were a tandem group that showed me you could share in the telling experience with someone else, and it took craftsmanship to do so. I even committed some stories to memory. Although I had taught myself with the tapes of their performances, nothing compared to live telling. A year later, I saw an advertisement for a storytelling performance by a local guild. I drove two hours to Cleveland, and from that day forward, I joined the group meeting once a month to both listen and tell with other members. However, I learned more than how to tell stories or the expected ways to tell. As I studied, I learned there were both implied and direct conduct rules for telling.

In writing this chapter, I have referred to the stories that helped me, but also addressed how my storytelling has been transformed. Initially, I followed strict rules, both implicit and explicit, as to what was considered good storytelling. This includes never interrupting the teller while he or she is sharing a story, the story must be told in one sitting, and only participate in the story when prompted to do so. I believe this, in some way, helped me improve my narrative delivery, but at the same time, was also a hindrance to my understanding of the full range of narrative and its potential when used for teaching. At the beginning, these rules helped me appreciate and improve as a teller. I worked on creating stories that could be told to an audience. I spent a great deal of time crafting the stories to mirror the storytellers on the tapes. However, this also rooted my thinking of how a story could be used. I dismissed stories as not workable that took more time, included interruptions, and involved improvisation. This type of honest reflection serves as a "doorway, an instrument of encounter, a place of public and private negotiations—where the goal is not just to empathize, but to attend" (Salverson 2001, 125).

From working with the guild, I learned how to stand or sit while telling stories; the importance of the beginning, middle, and end when composing a story for telling purposes; and the vital importance of catering a story for a specific audience. I not only learned storytelling, but the expectations of professional storytelling, including etiquette. First, a teller must tell before an audience. A story is not considered a told story unless shared with an audience. However, it could not simply be a gathering of people—the telling must happen when the teller had all the audience looking at him or her as he or she shared a story that could be told in one sitting. The audience was expected to listen to the story while the teller told. Second, a teller must never interrupt the flow of his or her story. What counted as interruption was equated to the curious questions a preschooler might ask when hearing a story. They ask about the story, tell the teller about new directions of the story, or ask questions where they are confused. In organized storytelling, the story is the experience, not the questions. The story is seen as something that must be told completely before a listening audience who can share comments. There are stories that encourage participation, but this is at the discretion of the teller.

THE INFLUENCE OF RUTH SAWYER

Considered to be a pioneer of professional storytelling, Ruth Sawyer was one of the first to define the art in relation to performance. She was a former librarian who left her work to become a professional storyteller. Her book, *The Way of the Storyteller* (1942), is still considered a classic text for beginning storytellers, and more advanced tellers keep it as reference. In it she says that storytelling is first and always a spoken story. "The instrument is our voice that we work with . . . the spoken language—words" (131). She says voice is the primary tool in telling, setting the tone for students to listen actively and not just passively participate while story is told. She concludes her chapter about "preparation" with the teller's goal: "To be able to create a story, to make it live during the moment of the telling, to arouse emotions—wonder, laughter, joy, amazement—this is the only goal a storyteller may have" (148).

I chose to challenge these traditional paradigms because in teaching using story, my goal was not simply to "arouse emotions"; instead, I wanted to use stories as a tool to introduce new material or reflect and extend an idea or concept. When working with students, in addition to telling fairy- and folktales—in organized storytelling—I often introduced personal and original tales. Sawyer did not see this as "tellable" material. In order for a story to be considered tellable, it must attract the audience's attention and be told in one sitting. Storyteller and author Kay Stone (1998) says that people who tell folk and fairy tales are involved in traditional storytelling, and these tellers are "nontheatrical." Instead, they are "authentic oral narrators" and extolled as "real" storytellers (4). She agrees with Sawyer, describing a typical storytelling event at a school or library as a form of organized storytelling.

> Organized storytelling usually took place during the day and in a pre-designated place with a somewhat formal arrangement: children sat on the floor or in chairs and the storyteller stood or sat alone in front of them, more from separating the single teller and the many acquiescent listeners. These sessions often lasted from thirty to sixty minutes and were scheduled in advance. (Stone 1998, 19)

Sawyer was one of the first librarians to quit her job to become a professional storyteller. She believed in the awesome ability of the storyteller. Like me, she learned it from listening.

> I once watched a drab and dirty tinker tell a story about the fairies at a Donegal crossroads. He gathered a crowd in no time. Words became living substance for all who listened. For the duration of the story nothing lived but the story, neither listeners nor storyteller. When it was over, we saw again that the tinker was drab and dirty, . . . haggling for trade; and we became . . . what we had been before. (Sawyer, 1942, 29)

Sawyer established respect and recognition for the art of storytelling, but almost fixed how stories could be conveyed in schools and libraries. She prized the unique way that stories operated when told aloud. She said that there is a kind of death to every story when it leaves the speaker and becomes impaled for all time on clay tablets or the written or printed page. To take it from the page, to create it again into living substance is the challenge. She also said that she was not concerned with how to tell stories or what stories to tell. She saw storytelling as a quest. In her book, she states, "It is a call to go questing, an urge to follow the way of the storyteller as pilgrims followed the way of Saint James in the Middle Ages, not for riches or knowledge or power, but that each might 'find something that transcends method, technique—the hows and the whys" (20). In this work, although I agree with many of Sawyer's methods, and some I question, I follow her advice, to find and explore how using stories transforms not only my students, but also me. She continues, "The art of storytelling lies within the storyteller, to be searched for, drawn out, make to grow" (26).

The way stories are told in organized storytelling is recorded in her book, *The Way of the Storyteller*. These are the same rules I learned as I discovered telling stories. However, I did break away from these rules because, when I was working with students, they had their own way of telling and sharing stories. I eventually learned to let go of these rules, in some cases reluctantly, finding new ways to use narratives for teaching. I also had to redefine the way I viewed story performance and story events. I detail this later in the chapter. I leaned away from only accepting performed stories, seeing performances in everyday storytelling as legitimate means of sharing.

STORYTELLING FOR LEARNING /BREAKING SAWYER'S RULES

When I started as a storyteller, I used stories to entertain and perform for an audience. However, when I began to teach, my story use transformed, shifting to a learning focus and outcome. I distinctly remember a student who worried about the gossiping she heard about herself and asked if she too should gossip. I turned to a Jewish story to help her. This is a story where a woman has to pick up feathers in a pillow on a windy day at the Rabbi's request. Before, it was easy to spread them around, but to pick them up was a different matter. The Rabbi said so it was the same with gossip. My story was used to illuminate the student's choices. I referred another student seeking understanding for her cultural background as a member of the Cherokee tribe to old folktales and personal narratives of Cherokees to discover past heritages. She did not want or need a pleasing story, but a way to connect to her personal history.

Another notion of Sawyer and organized storytelling is that storytelling stands on its own. It cannot be combined with other teaching, such as art, history, math, or English. As many storytellers informed me, holistic storytellers simply tell stories, without props, and no extended learning. They believe the story speaks on its own. As noted, Sawyer (1942) objects to using story in combination with other arts or learning: "I am decrying . . . the telling of stories to impart information or to train in any specified direction. The sooner this unhampering be accomplished the more positive and direct will be the approach to our goal, which I take to be creative" (32). As a teacher, I had always used story in combination with other learning practices. When I first taught British literature, I soon realized my students were not fascinated with the text as it was written. For them, Old English and medieval England were barriers to their understanding. The works of Sir Walter Raleigh, Edmund Spencer, and William Shakespeare did not mirror their own lives. I used story to help students connect and understand poetry and stories. When we were studying pastoral poetry, I created a modern story environment to share student reworkings of the poem, in this case, the drive-in theater. Students shared love sonnets and "A Nymph's Reply to the Shepherd" in a story vernacular that included contemporary language and behaviors. We compared the original story that was told with the one they created from modern times. When we contemporized stories, words, and settings, students then wanted to learn the original language and plotlines. Sawyer would have disagreed: "It has been a kind of horror that I watched eager and intelligent young minds being thumb-screwed under the belief that storytelling could not stand alone as an art that its reason for existence depended on some extraneous motive" (Sawyer 1962, revised, 1942, 32). In schools, effective teaching increased learning, but in the world of professional storytellers, this is not a concern. Storytellers do not concern themselves with the learning, but instead with the story experience. The main question to be answered was, Is the story pleasing for the listeners? The listening experience was what was required in order to learn. Therefore, in order to use stories to teach students, I needed to use stories not only for a listening experience, but also for a learning one.

In my first job at Brunswick High School in Ohio, I taught American literature, British literature, and speech. I struggled to find how best to manage my learning environments. I soon discovered story invited students to listen to my teaching. I purposefully shaped my instruction using stories to build classroom community. On Fridays, I designed stories to teach the British literature curriculum developing our own version of Chaucer's *Canterbury Tales*, called the Brunswick Tales. As Barthes (1974) states, "the goal of literary work (of literature as work) is to make the reader no longer a consumer, but a producer of text" (3). Students created their own stories, oral and written. They performed their Brunswick Tales only after preparing them for a journal manuscript. When we performed and shared our stories, we began to know one another better. Instead of traditional reading, such as chapter readings, we read to design stories to share in groups with the class. In my British literature class, we rewrote and performed *Romeo and Juliet*, telling our own story. In my speech classes, students gave speeches influenced by a biography of a famous person. Instead of simply reading the biography, we created and performed first-person, biographical stories. I can still remember the three Hitlers, and how each student had a different explanation for his death. This encouraged much debate and more narratives.

Initially, I worried about using narrative in my lessons. I was unsure how storytelling fit into the academic disciplines I was teaching. I was trained to use rigid lesson plans to introduce subjects, not story. The lesson plan included allocations of time-based activities and preplanned questions, and, generally, each minute was designed and created by me. It was not a place to tell a story and build from students' interest when developing curriculum from the story. When I first started teaching, I thought my students would question my story-based pedagogy. This did not happen; in fact, they asked for more. Teaching using story worked. I recognized my particular leaning toward narratives. It became almost a reflex to look for how I could address a lesson using story or story performance. If it was poetry, I determined how it could be performed like storytelling. If it was nonfiction, I looked at how story could be developed from the essay. Although I worried my students would ask for less story-based work, they never did. I did not use them in every lesson, but I did lean toward narrative as a teaching method. Because my students responded to story, I worried less about disciplining my students and began to build my curriculum to include the student discovery of narrative. In fact, disciplinary problems became less and less because we used narrative not as a form of control, but as a way to invite students in the process of learning. When I assigned poetry, students created a narrative outlet to perform what they had studied. When reflecting, I gave students a good deal of freedom to work within the set parameters. Narrative provided students a way to talk about the literature and themselves. They became producers of the text, which included deciding what they considered significant in their learning (Heathcote 1984).

At Hanford High School in 1995, I had the honor of serving as the first high school storytelling teacher in the country where my role as a storyteller changed forever. As a classroom teacher, what was my role? Could I still be a storyteller if I did not traditionally perform stories? When I began teaching in 1990, I was the storyteller, and students were the story listeners. The roles, however, would reverse as I listened to the students' stories. I draw upon a telling experience to illustrate. When I told the Cinderella variant known as Little Burnt Face, an Algonquian tale, I used often in the classroom, I was the only teller. Following the rules of organized storytelling, no one interrupted. However, left to wonder, when I served as the sole teller, was I unintentionally silencing my students' stories? As Dyson and Genishi (1994) caution, "stories, and therefore aspects of children's lives, can be silenced if listeners (including teachers and peers) do not appreciate the diverse ways stories are crafted and the range of experiences they tap" (4). Since I served as the only teller, how could I craft the telling of stories to include students' voices?

After sharing a told story of Sir Gawain and the Green Knight, I asked students to share their own versions of a tellable story. As Dyson and Genishi (1994) share, "the storytelling self is a social self, who declares and shapes important relationships through the mediating power of words" (5). Storytelling is a social act; it is a way to bring a group together to listen to each other. However, as the teacher, I could deter how social students were in the storytelling event or experience. I needed to let go and allow more interlocutors in the making and telling of the stories. It was not enough to tell the story to the class; I needed a better way to increase the relationship between the story and the tellers. As we continued to share, when students started to tell together, I introduced tandem telling so they could socially engage not only in the telling process, but in the sharing of the tales as well. By working together, they could share ideas and reinterpret text. Although I did not have the formal language then, I was advocating a sociocultural approach to learning, which is not random, but learned (Vygotsky, 1978). According to Jeannie Oakes and Martin Lipton (2003), "Relationships that can enhance or inhibit learning are organized or structured in families, schools, the workplace, and so on. In other words, when we organize a classroom and the interactions within, we are structuring learning" (81). I explored learning derived from teaching involving more tellers, which went against the rules of organized storytelling. I simply wanted to work with my students to ease their fears, so I encouraged them to partner with another student storyteller.

As expected, students felt more comfortable telling with another person. Many of my students in California were second-language learners, showing much apprehension when telling alone in front of the class. When partnered with another teller, they engaged in the social sharing of ideas for their stories. They tried many styles and were not stilted from lack of practice. For example, many students chose to tell an old Appalachian folktale, No News, which lends nicely to tandem telling as an effective introduction. Although they were telling socially with one another, the words were not in a social context, and there were no deviations in the words to be used with this type of tandem telling. The words were scripted and memorized. Although, socially, they negotiate their posture, timing, and pausing, who tells what, their word choices were exactly dictated by the text. Even though students do deviate when telling, they are somewhat confined by the structured back-and-fourth of the conversation. I not only wanted to find another way to use story to help students not only share a story together using a written text, but to find meaning through their own language choices and even frame new stories based upon these choices.

I was impressed with Jonatha and Harold Wright, Tandem Tellers and Story Quilters, whose storytelling style used more improvisation and playful banter instead of a defined script. I had hoped to incorporate these concepts within my own classroom. In improvisation, tellers work from a "story line," knowing the story well enough to play as they tell and create. However, as I learned from a personal conversation with an Upper Skagit elder, Vi Hilbert, first know the bones of the story and then, and only then, can you add the flesh. For example, if students are "playing" with the telling of Jack and the Beanstalk, they may find new ways of telling, perhaps making the mother more pronounced discovering she is really a rapper. They are free to experiment with language in rap verse to develop plot.

When those involved in narrative interactions actively participate as both tellers and recipients, they exercise their entitlement

to co-author a narrative. When a narrative concerns a lived experience, co-authors impact the understanding of that experience. It is
not only a narrative but also a life or a history that is collaboratively
constructed. Narrative is a sense-making activity; it is also a primary vehicle for retaining experiences in memory. Entitlement to
co-tell a narrative is then a powerful right, encompassing past, present, future, as well as imagined worlds (Ochs and Capps 2001, 201).

When students start with a story line, instead of a full story, they
can introduce their own experiences into the story work. Each new
step, from solo to tandem telling to improvisational stories, creates
a social context for learning and working with students. The more
students are engaged in co-authorship, the more they learn with
their own language. Unlike the type of tandem telling where students are provided with the words, with story lines, students can
use improvisation to choose the words, how they are said, and how
they are performed. They can do this in a social context, working
with other students. They co-author the construction of the story,
discussing how they see the story in relation to how others see it.

As authors, children may thus learn that they do not own their
text's meaning, but they are responsible for that text nonetheless,
and they are responsible through it (Bakhtin 1981, 280).

Through what they chose to say and chose not to say, they
respond to the world around them (Dyson 1997). Initially, I asked
my students to memorize lines when working with a partner, but
soon afterwards, I employed more of an improvisational assignment for tandem telling. In fact, in my first year of teaching, I called
the best-selling co-author Kim Kirberger of *Chicken Soup for the
Teenage Soul* and convinced her we could produce a video of stories
before the first book was published. I was sent an earlier version of
the book, and I remember being frustrated alongside my students
because we had to stick to the script. I knew my students could learn
much more if they had some latitude to reinterpret the work, so I
convinced the authors to permit us some leeway. They allowed us to
alter about 10 percent of the actual text. During the process, which

took more than one thousand hours of volunteer time after school, I questioned what I was teaching. What were my students learning from this story work? Applying Vygotsky's (1978) sociocultural perspectives on learning, I now see students were confined because the language could not be changed. The scripted language stilted or at least stalled them, and they were told to not deviate from it more than 10 percent. They were confined because they were not creating or involved in the making of the work, but instead only in the performance of it. Although I recognized the interpretation with voice and body, there were more choices. However, my students were new to understanding performance. They showed frustration in learning and doing the same thing over and over again. They were not free to make choices because they were stuck on learning the script. In fact, we were way over schedule because many of them would not memorize. We had little time to explore choices in the work because we spent more time just learning the words.

In order for my students to learn, they needed be able to co-author the work. I had taught them the art of telling stories and making choices; this was not what I taught. They learned from me that they co-author a tale by making choices in telling it in this way. We could have made meaning together. As Dyson (1997) referring to Vygotsky, illustrates, "When children's meaning-making, their imagining of pleasurable worlds, is 'completed' in words, the ideological 'force' of those words may reverberate in their classroom communities and, simultaneously, in their own sense or consciousness of themselves as social agents in those communities" (129). Students need to be involved in the co-creative process. When students seek the help of others in creating and performing narratives, narratives can take on new directions. From the time children learn to play, they want to control the play. Having a script can restrict this sense of play.

Alternatively, the would-be narrator may seek others' assistance in developing a point of view on events. While even the simplest predication conveys a point of view—through choice of grammatical form, lexical content, prosody, stylistic register, dialect, language, and the like, narratives have the potential to build more elaborate perspectives, cause-effect relations, and implications (Ochs and Capps 2001, 114).

As I reflect upon my work as a storytelling teacher, I need to ask, Did I place more value in telling than the making of story? How important was it to perform the stories? Can one learn from the act of creating stories? Which method supports a more sociocultural approach to teaching? King (1993) explains the value when students are creating stories; can this be mirrored when students are telling stories? My own teaching experience has shown that sharing stories and making drama help to make the abstract more concrete and diverse facts more understandable and arouse interest in learning as students become engrossed, not only in the story itself, but in the cultural or social context in which it is told. How much of a cultural and social understanding was provided by my focus on story performance? Which place, storymaking or storytelling, allowed for co-authoring? In other words, what would I emphasize in my teaching, the storytelling, and/or the storymaking? Before teaching, I was a performer. I saw value in a told performance. In fact, I had a bias toward performance. I have to admit my bias may have limited my understanding of how narratives could be used for teaching. My leaning toward narrative as performance tilted my teaching toward performance. This is hard to acknowledge because much of my work was oriented toward this.

When reflecting, I also need to be vulnerable (Behar 1996). It is hard to admit I spent time focusing my teaching on performance. As a result, I recall the discomfort of my students in California, especially those who were migrant students, where they tried to slip into the shadows, and how I spent extra effort trying to not only create a story, but also perform it. Although I did work hard to create a nonthreatening environment for performance sharing with the class, I have to humbly realize now sometimes the storymaking would be enough. Students did not have to perform their stories to be learning from them. There is value in storymaking. From this, I learned to establish a differentiation between storymaking and storytelling. In turn, performed stories can be a place of learning, but in order to elevate what I am teaching, students should have more choices in the improvisational nature of performing them. In other words, I need to be less of a director and instead allow the stories to take shape from a sociocultural method of learning. Initially, I concentrated on the performance, but as we worked together, I in turn, trusted my students to develop their story work together.

I think of the times when my students were collecting ghost stories and the spirited conversations we had about what they discovered. The students went into our small town of Hanford, California, interviewed residents about ghosts, and reported back what they found. This discussion was rich, but sometimes in my teaching, I would rush these invaluable conversations to make room for the performance. It is also humbling to realize as a professional storyteller that I often reduced the tellership and tellability for my students. Since I was making the decisions about what was told and how it was told, I reduced their level of participation and limited the topics. In sharing Little Burnt Face, I could have taught the same principles if we co-created a native tale based upon nonfiction resources. In fact, this would have allowed me an extended opportunity to talk about the culture and tradition of the Algonquin tribe. Although I researched the tale when creating it for performance, this would allow the students to actively engage in learning about a culture that was not their own. This in and of itself could have been a powerful learning experience.

When I served as the primary teller, if I directed the stories, my students followed. These are times in my teaching when I should have shared in the telling instead of placing the spotlight on my telling. Although my intent was to direct my students to learn from oral telling, at times, it might have been better to build a community of sharing instead.

Indeed, these researchers (students) are vulnerable to the criticism that they are self-indulgent and that they air dirty laundry that nobody wants to see. Yet they ground these practices in the idea that researchers need to understand themselves if they are to understand how they interpret narrators' stories. Readers need to understand researcher's stories (about their intellectual and personal relationships with narrators as well as with the cultural phenomena at hand) if readers are to understand narrator's stories (Tierney 2002; Tierney and Lincoln 1997).

I was always looking for how story could be told, and instead, I needed to look at how story, performance or not, could be used to enhance learning. Upon reflection, I have learned there are other ways to successful shared telling. As Langellier and Peterson (2004) note, "At a minimum, performance involves a two-step process of 'taking' and 'making' experience for someone: first, as an embodied listener at work in the world, the storyteller takes his or her consciousness of experience and 'in turn' makes it an experience of consciousness for the audience" (3). Can something be performed when it is in the making process? How valuable is highly performed storytelling and more casual storytelling in everyday lives? Bauman (1978, 8) argues all speech is an event. In his sense, the interaction of speaking, the involvement of different participants, their roles, and the negotiations of their relationships are always events in themselves. He suggests we understand such events, which are on a continuum of more and less performed. He goes on to say that in everyday conversation, a narrative requires a longer turn at talk and therefore is always somewhat of a performance, even if it is very informal. He also argues that when a narrative is spoken, it is performed. In my classroom, what kind of events provided the most effective teaching, formal or informal performance? When teaching using a more formal performance storytelling lens, the event changes. As Langellier and Peterson (2004) describe,

> When we participate in storytelling, whether as storytellers or audiences, we re-enact storytelling as a conventionalized form of communication as well as collaborate in the production of a unique story

or performance. This storytelling event recites, recalls, and reiterates previous storytelling events in general and in particular. In brief, storytelling is socially and culturally reflexive. (4)

One of the strongest lessons in my teaching was not performed as a told story or prepared and presented for an audience. This was using narrative to promote questions and inquiry, not performance. This experience showed me performance is not always audience-centered. Some narratives require a different kind of participation and are less for an audience and more of an interlocutor (Ochs and Capps 2001). Each member is involved in the conversation. Audience-centered storytelling involves identifiable tellers and listeners. Typically, a solo teller shares a story with a group of listeners. However, what happens when there is no audience, but there is a group of students and a teaching model using narrative to question and consider possibilities? In traditional storytelling, in order for it to be storytelling, it must have "the teller, the tale, and the listener" (Lipman 1999). However, if the listening is more active than passive, it does not occur in "once upon a time" time, but instead in the present moment, can it still be considered storytelling?

This is an example where I needed to redefine the term "storytelling," to see the storymaking process as a form of storytelling. Tales were being exchanged, interrupted, changed, and evaluated. Many tellers, instead of one, were telling stories where some were complete, some abandoned, and some only shared in fragments. However, these experiences involved the components of storytelling, tales, tellers, and listeners. It only lacked an audience, but it still was considered storytelling. Strip away the audience, and stories can still be performed.

Storytelling was definitely evident when the high school janitor came into my creative writing class to show me what he had found on the roof above my classroom. In a wadded-up bundle of blankets were baby clothes, textbooks, teenage girl clothes, and food items. The last item was a journal. As I read it, I discovered that seven years previously, a student had written the journal while she and her new baby lived on the high school roof. There were sporadic entries of her life as a runaway. Without planning to do so, as my next class entered the classroom, I shared the journal, and we discovered her story together. As I read it out loud, we learned that her boyfriend had beaten her, and she was too scared to go home. She shared how hard it was to live on her own but did not mention living on the roof. I did not know what to do with the journal. Some students chose to write about how they would have finished the journal if they had been her. Others wrote in role as the student, boyfriend, or even the father. After class, some students expressed real concern to help find out more about the story and take action to help return the journal to the owner and even report the abuse. We never performed this story, but instead used it to help build upon each other's questions and ideas. Although it was not formally performed, stories were being told from this experience. We spent four class periods with some of the best writing, discussion, and planning from the journal.

During this time, we were sharing stories—stories of the possible and stories to fill in the gaps left by the journal. At no time did we perform our interpretation; instead we were involved in the narrative of this girl and her baby. Students even began to share their own stories. As Benjamin (1969) states, "the storyteller takes what he tells from experience—his own or that reported by others. He, in turn, makes the experience of those who are listening to his tale" (87). Clearly, this was another effective way to use narrative. When students share narratives, they take risks, which can lead to more sharing. In other words, when the stories are told, they can be shared with others. This young lady's journal invited students to tell their own stories of hardship, what is was like being a Latino teenager and how parents react if you have a baby when you are a teen. We actively talked about this story and wrote about it, talked about our ideas, told stories, and wrote more.

At a different time, a nonperformance narrative surfaced when I taught an Opportunity class for students who were labeled "disadvantaged" in their learning in some way or simply had frequently been in trouble. The principal said this class received its name because the students had more opportunities in jail than school. It became their last chance to stay in school. I worked with these students during an extended block of time. The assistant principal believed they needed "hard discipline." I tried this for a short period of time with no success. However, these students, like the students who shared during the reading of the journal, needed a place to voice their frustrations. I opened this classroom, not a place to perform stories, but as a place to share them. As a class, we read the book *Holes* by Louis Sachar. Students began to question the text. They did not understand why it was so hard to dig holes, so I arranged for them to do so themselves behind the bus garage. This experiment created an investment for my students. We were able to listen not only to their stories, but to the counterstories they created through their own experiences. In essence, students who are engaged in crime repeat the crimes without remorse because many people, even school officials such as the school police officer, subscribe to these available narratives. They see "troubled" students. "Available narratives" (Shuman 1986) are also referred to as master narratives. According to Nelson (2001), master narratives are "the stories found lying about in our culture" (6). Nelson goes on to say,

> Master narratives are often archetypal, consisting of stock plots and readily recognizable character types, and we use them not only to make sense of our experiences (Nisbett and Ross, 1980) but also to justify what we do (MacIntyre, 1984). As the repositories of common norms, master narratives exercise a certain authority over our moral imaginations and play a role in informing our moral intuitions. (6)

I have to admit I fought against what people told me about the students who were enrolled in my Opportunity class. Many school officials and students labeled them as apathetic, crooks, or lazy. However, when I taught using the story of *Holes*, we used the stories in the book to discuss the dominant narratives of their lives with the counterstories they told about their lives. As Nelson (2001) relates, "I claimed that the stock plots and readily recognizable character types of master narratives characterize groups of peoples in certain ways, thereby cultivating and maintaining norms for the behavior of the people who belong to these groups and weighting the ways others will or won't see them" (106).

In fact, when we were beginning to dig holes behind the bus garage in the blistering California heat, similar to the blazing heat of the novel in Nevada, the assistant principal, who saw the students, who were not to be anywhere except in the Opportunity classroom, demanded to know why they were there. Even though they were with a teacher, the narrative he supported when talking with them was that of troublemaker. He demanded to know who gave them permission to be there. I stepped in and loudly listed all the people who gave us permission, including the principal and the grounds officials. Still, I was shut down. I yelled a bit more, explaining the lesson that I was attempting to teach. The assistant principal would hear none of it. I quietly picked up our shovels and returned to class. The students left for their next class. I felt defeated. This administrator had seen the students as troublemakers. However, the next day each student came in and, in some way, said, "Cordi went up against the man. You have to respect Cordi." After that day, we had more open authentic conversations, less about labels and more about real world experiences.

Although my students were lumped together as "Opportunity students," they all had different stories to tell. This is where Nelson's idea of the narrative counterstory comes into play. Nelson (2001) says that the counter story "positions itself against a number of master narratives" (6). I will never forget when a freshman student, Vanessa, came to my class and told me she was too little to be jumped into a gang. She began to share with me how on her block she had to join a gang; there was no choice. She was worried she might die or at least be badly injured because, in order to be jumped into a gang, you had to march in a makeshift parade while your gang beat you with fists and sticks. The master or available narrative stated a person who joined a gang was up to no good. However, Vanessa told a counterstory about being forced to join the gang. The master narrative would encourage her to move, so the problem would go away. When I asked if this was a choice, she said no, her family was too poor. According to Nelson (2001), the counterstory works in two steps. The first step "is to identify the fragments of master narratives that have gone into the construction of an oppressive identity, noting how these fragments misrepresent persons . . . and situations." The second step is to "re-tell the story about the person or the group to which the person belongs in such a way to make visible the morally relevant details that master narratives suppressed. If the re-telling is successful, the group members will stand reveled as respect worthy agents" (Nelson 2001, 7). I retold Vanessa's story to her without judgment. I listened to her story and the truth of it. I did not give her a long lecture on why gangs are bad; I instead tried to offer advice. I left the students to take what they could from hearing it. As Sawyer (1942) said of Johanna, an Irish nurse teller she learned from, "There was the tale—I could take it or leave it; and I always took it" (18). I shared this advice based on what I was given for the situation. I did not gather it from platitudes that one might find on a brochure against gangs, but instead from the narrative Vanessa shared. She had the right to her narrative even though it was one that hurt to tell. I even explored various interpretations, positioning her not as making a morally degrading choice, but exploring choices she had available under her constraints. After we talked, Vanessa did not show up for three days. I was worried, but when I saw her, she whispered, "I am alright." I did alert the guidance counselor but respected her silence in her story. As Nelson (2001) states, a secondary aim of the counterstory is "to alter, where necessary, an oppressed person's perception of herself" (7). Vanessa was able to see her story and not tell it in a way she needed to communicate. Her silence told a story. Her lack of words spoke about her situation.

There is another dominant narrative being shared with me as a teacher who is expected to advocate school rules over student stories. When we read *Holes*, my students advocated the need to use frank language and discuss events in their life that were not in a standardized curriculum. As they discussed the stories, they became more and more answerable (Bakhtin 1990) as to how they were positioned and how they identified with these positions. Their stories helped give them voice. I slowly allowed it. I gave in; I created a space for them to tell their stories the way they would share them with their peers. This included language of abuse and morally disrespectful words such as "wetback." These words would never be included in standard curriculum instruction. I resisted the dominant narrative that a teacher is the police of language. Instead, I listened. As I shared my own story of being jumped on three separate occasions, students felt comfortable sharing their counterstories of struggling between staying in school and staying out of trouble, how many probationary notices they received, and in some cases, how much time they had spent in "juvie." I listened as they shared stories of police officials who labeled them as "troublemakers" or school administrators who treated them differently than other students. These conversations drifted into further conversation about parents, home life, and gang stereotyping. I had been taught to put an end to all swearing and anger in my classrooms. However, this time I let them talk, and talk they did, learning more about their worldviews and understandings, encouraging them to use the language of their peers.

Ochs and Capps (2001) introduce an interactive definition of narrative concerned with personal, everyday, or what they call "living" narratives. "Personal narrative is a way of using language or another symbolic system to imbue life events with a temporal and logical order, to demystify them and establish coherence across past, present, and as yet unrealized experience" (1–2).

TELLERSHIP

As noted in the descriptive examples throughout this chapter, personal narratives can be found in the classroom. Ochs and Capps (2001) examine these narrative dimensions, including tellership. When I changed my own tellership focus to high, involving others in discussion, my students responded to my teaching. My teaching improved. As mentioned earlier, tellership refers to the involvement level the "conversational partners" have with each other within the narrative (24). In all three illustrations, tellership belonged to both the students and me as we collaboratively shared in the learning. Together we discussed the student's journal; examined the depth of *Holes*, physically and figuratively; and explored ghost histories. I changed my role from primary teller to "collaborative interlocutor" (Ochs and Capps 2001, 352), inviting students to share their stories and questions. In the case of my Opportunity class, I even suspended normal school rules, inviting stories of the students' culture and identity. I recognized Bakhtin's (1990) view that language is never neutral; it is filled with many voices: "The author does not speak in a given language (from which he distances himself to a greater or lesser degree) but he speaks, as it were through language, a language that has somehow more or less materialized, become objectified, that he merely ventriloquotes" (Bakhtin 1981, 299–300).

TELLABILITY

The next dimension from Ochs and Capps (2001) is tellability, which refers to how relevant narratives are to the teller and interlocutors. "A narrator may relay an unusual incident that captures the audience's interest and appreciation and draws them into his or her perspective. Alternatively, in other conversational narratives, conversational partners are grilled about their day's activities and reel out what happened reluctantly, without bothering to dress up as particularly important" (34) In all three narrative events, the stories are important to the students. They felt connected not only to their narratives, but also to the narratives of their peers. I can tell this from the conversations they had with me and their classmates. In the case of the journal, the unfinished story increased their personal investment. I remember known and unknown students coming in to see the journal after class and discussing it with their friends. They argued what to do with it long after class was over. With the Opportunity class, story invited real life comparisons with fiction. I did not create the curriculum alone; we co-created through our inquiry, posing questions and resolving concerns.

One student who wanted to talk about alternative methods of correcting the behavior of the students shared about the places he was in and how people treated him. This led to the class talking about how adults should treat teenagers. When I increased the tellability of these narrative events, my teaching improved because instead of hearing told stories, we were sharing within the narratives experiences. In fact, student inquiry and curiosity guided the direction of our learning. In these three examples, the story events created transformative learning within the classroom.

> . . . transformations mean progressing from an incomplete story to one that is more complete and compelling. We do this by establishing first the connectedness or coherence that moves the storyline along through time. Next comes the direction of the story, the goal or the point of it all. With the goal established events are selected, rejected, or transformed and take on significance that they would not have otherwise possessed. (Gudmundsdottir 1995, 34)

EMBEDDEDNESS

Embeddedness, the third dimension of narrative, describes the connection between narratives. Ochs and Capps (2001) define it as "the extent to which a personal narrative is an entity unto itself, separate from prior, concurrent and subsequent discourse, is related to turn organization, thematic content, and rhetorical structuring" (36). When I tell a told story such as "Little Burnt Face," is it detached from other narratives? According to Ochs and Capps (2001), this would have low embeddedness when compared to the ghost stories mentioned above or the teaching with the *Holes* text. The ghost story narratives often drew from told narratives shared within the Hanford community over many years. Students were able to compare and contrast the authenticity of these with other residents who were claimed or unclaimed ghost tellers. As they shared their tales, students were able to trace Hanford's history and development. They would tell a ghost story about how someone haunts the railroad, and students would travel on their own to the historical society and not only find out about the possible ghost, but why the railroad was important as well. They shared this with the class. In the Opportunity class, students experienced first-hand how to dig a hole, relating the experience directly to their own lives. A told story in teaching does not occur again after the lesson is completed. It can, but not often because the story is geared around the lesson. However, in the classroom, narratives were often referred to again and again. We went back to the journal because it created significant meaning for all of us. Interest piqued around the school for the ghost stories. Students who were not even in my class would stop in my classroom to determine the authenticity of the ghost stories. When I look at how stories are used for teaching, I need to see how I can embed with other conversations and stories relevant to the students.

I am suggesting that high embeddedness is useful for all classroom interactions. "Embeddedness" is a useful term because it is not restricted to contextual relevance or familiarity. Rather, a teacher can introduce a completely unfamiliar story and provide high embeddedness that makes the learning relevant. At the same time, it is a risky teaching strategy because it goes beyond the structure of the lesson and allows for dialogic inquiry. The teacher is not necessarily in an authoritative role, and the interaction is open to critical discourse. You cannot anticipate the stories and turn them in as part of a lesson plan, nor can an administrator objectively evaluate them.

My larger question is whether there is any dimension of narrative that might have low embeddedness and still engage the learner. Some solo tellers argue even the solo art of telling is a creative process that engages listeners. From a teaching standpoint, when students are co-authors, or what Freire (1970) calls critical co-investigators, the dialogic dimension of learning is more visible. We might consider how high performance and low embeddedness contribute to a transformative environment that transports students into the world created by the solo teller. I would argue that such telling is actually very highly embedded because the storyteller creates a highly embedded context for all participants. James Moffet (1983) might disagree with this because he believes story is by its very nature relegated to the past; drama speaks to the present with a hint to the future.

LINEARITY

Narrative's fourth dimension is linearity, which "concerns the extent to which narratives of personal experience depict events as transpiring in a single, closed, temporal or causal path or, alternatively, in diverse, open, uncertain paths" (Ochs and Capps 2001, 83). In the stories I told or performed, I knew the destination, and in turn, focused my teaching around the significant moments. When I designed the "Little Burnt Face" activities with story, I designed them not around open-ended questions, but more on retelling or refocusing what we had to work from in the story. However, with the found journal, as a class, we questioned every day. Students presented their own theories as to how the writer ended up living on the school's roof. Clearly, the unfinished journal provided a context for further story generation from multiple voices and perspectives. Without a definitive closure, further inquiry created both possible pasts and futures. Students were quite invested in helping her, so I never knew what they might introduce into the story. I left the class discussion unstructured and open so we could explore our choices together to unfold this narrative. How could I create less of a traditional narrative order with a structured beginning, middle, and end, and more of an exploration like the ghost stories or the student on the roof? Once again, I needed to let go of my traditional understanding of story and see my teaching from a social, open-ended method. I needed to structure the stories so my students could be involved in their composition and understanding.

MORAL STANCE

The last dimension of narrative is moral stance. As I am quoted, in *Moral of the Story*, "We spend too much time telling students to 'Just Say No' instead of seeing the story that comes from saying yes. It is time that the real value of storytelling for children, young adults and adults is realized, so we can value our own choices and help others make theirs" (Norfolk and Norfolk 1999, 3).

Is there a better way to introduce morals when using story to teach? As Maxine Greene (1973) argues, "the teacher who wishes to be more than functionary cannot escape the value problem or the difficult matter of moral choice" (181). As a storyteller, I recently traveled to an out-of-state performance where a group of students created a play called, "Second Chances." The students performed this play, which chronicles the life of a student who is involved in drugs and dies but is granted a second opportunity. The play was highly religious with a moralizing stance: "don't do drugs" and "God says drugs are wrong." As I watched, I remember thinking how disconnected the play was to the students' real lives. These students lived in challenging neighborhoods where drugs were present daily.

Instead, morals could be developed by opening questions rather than sharing dogmatic platitudes. How can using narratives work to create a space for students to wrestle with these issues instead of giving conclusions on drugs? Can story be used in a better way to help teach moral understandings? Educational philosopher Nell Noddings and Paul J. Shore (1998) suggest that stories can be used as the "starting point for critical thinking and the philosophical study of morality and ethics" (613). However, like the example above, this is why I strongly object to the systematic story advocated by the DARE program. Ochs and Capps (2001) discuss moral stance: "Narratives of personal experience do not present objective, comprehensive accounts of events but rather perspective on events. Rooted in community and tradition, moral stance is a disposition towards what is good or valuable and how one ought to live in the world" (45). Keeping this in mind, I think if the students had helped design the play, then they could tell the story of their lives or at least how their peers faced these issues. It was quite obvious from the reactions of student actors that they were distant from the material. Their lines were given in a rote manner. However, later these same performers mesmerized me when they showed their step-dance work. They clearly had designed this. The other stories did not connect to them, and there was clearly a distance between the words and the performance. Perhaps it was a difference in medium—one was scripted learning and the other could build on improvisational choices.

When I tell "Little Burnt Face," I try to present choices the Algonquian people might have made—preserving nature, respecting the spirit world, and valuing individual differences. In the nonperformance work, such as the journal or ghost stories, we did not nullify or criticize the decisions or moral choices presented; we accepted them. As Greene (1973) says of teachers, but the same thing can be said of students,

> Involved individuals have to make the moral choices which are ordinarily specific. The more sensitive teachers are to the demands of the

process or justification, the more explicit they are about the norms that govern their actions, the more personally engaged they are in assessing surrounding circumstances and potential consequences, the more "ethical" they will be; and we cannot ask much more. (221)

We considered comparing them with our own choices and lives, creating a dialogic space where each voice was answerable (Bakhtin 1990). As I reflect, I reevaluate and rethink how I can present and support more perspectives in my telling. Better yet, how can I share the telling, so other students are not only listening, but telling their work? For example, I caution other educators about programs like Character Counts, where students study a value for a week only. I did not like how one moral was emphasized and then forgotten for another. What is lost in emphasizing one moral is, among other things, a student's opportunity to address other issues. Just like the scripted speeches, there are only the words provided that can be used, but when using story to discuss morals and not choose them for students, students can agree, disagree, bring in personal perspectives, and evaluate the choices of others along with their own.

Some also argue that stories create a form of immorality simply by hearing them. I turn to Sawyer: "I have been told that the story of 'The Three Bears' conditions a child to fear: that 'Red Riding Hood' conditions against grandmothers; that 'Jack and the Beanstalk' induces a fixation for stealing. And well do I remember the young mother who once came to me asking for a list of stories which would keep Jerry from running away" (33). I need to re-examine what kind of choice, if any, an actual performance of telling allows for students. In stories, we often polarize the choices, but in discovery, the choices are open. Again, I need to examine how I redefine storytelling. Instead, I need to see how I can adopt an "ethic of caring" (Noddings 1986). For Noddings (1986), the central issue is not one choice or moralizing principle, but instead the relationship. Natural caring—the sort of response made when we want to care for another (a loved one, a baby, a sick friend)—establishes the ideal for ethical caring, and ethical caring imitates the ideal in its efforts to institute, maintain, or reestablish natural caring. "Persons guided by an ethic of caring do not ask whether it is their duty to be faithful . . . [R]ather, for them fidelity to persons is fidelity; indeed, fidelity is a quality of the relation and not merely an attribute of an individual's moral agent's behavior or character" (Noddings 1986, 385). I need to present stories but be open to the frank discussions of my students so we can establish and open spaces where we can discuss ideas without judgment. Narrative and drama are tools where this can be done, but only by establishing a nonthreatening environment in which to do so.

How can I help create the spaces where student voices are heard? These experiences left me to wonder in the classroom: How often are students invited to tell their stories? What have we not heard? I asked one of my students, Maggie, to report to me any time her honors class teacher asked her opinion. She came in frustrated after three weeks and said to me, "Mr. Cordi, either I don't understand the assignment, or I can't do it. Outside of this class, no one has asked me what I think."Langellier and Peterson (2004) say, "The emphasis on storytelling performance conceptualizes narrative as act, event, and discourse—a site for understanding and intervening in the ways culture produces, maintains, and transforms relations of identity and difference" (3). When we worked with the journal, I was not listening as a teacher. During this social and collaborative discovery, I heard the students not as students who wanted to do well academically, but as students who cared about the girl behind the journal. When one of my Latina students expressed a need to know if she was Latina, we talked about the importance of family relations within Latino homes. It would have been easy to lump Latino behaviors from this journal, but this was something I wanted to avoid. We did not use this journal to stereotype a culture, but instead, to share a personal narrative. I needed to mediate the conversation away from this type of thinking and move toward the personal and reflective account that was shared in the journal. I remember some of my "rough-edged" students talking about their need to break away. This was not standards-based teaching or typical academic discourse.

In my years of teaching, I have seen student voices fade more and more from the curriculum. In this story about a found journal, my students asked authentic questions because they wanted to hear the young lady's story. They invested in the power of listening deeply to this story. They did not listen because they were receiving a grade, but instead because they cared. In this national craze, which increases every year, to standardize the curriculum, we are losing the immense power that comes from listening to and with our students. We work so everyone has the same curriculum regardless of where they are in the country. However, I suggest that stories like this student's journal increase our students' attention and investment into learning. These are the stories that are becoming lost or repressed. These stories invite learning. They are not something you find in a standardized test.

It is also important to note my role as a storytelling teacher, I did not pass judgment on the girl who wrote the journal. Instead, I shared the story, and my students listened. I did not draw on prescribed strategies to enhance comprehension; instead, I built the curriculum based on their questions. I listen to hear the story. There are many reasons to hear stories. Students voice pain after learning they have or someone close to them has cancer or a student shares that he came from a troubled family or still another student proudly tells how she invented something new. Are our students prepared to hear these stories? Do they have the unique listening skills to hear them? This can only occur if they hear these types of stories. This is something we should be practicing and teaching with our students.

Students also not only need to listen to the stories, but they need to engage in the stories of difference without judgment. As we standardize the curriculum, are we not erasing the stories of struggle, resistance, and need for identity? Students need to develop these skills to listen to these stories, and a prepackaged curriculum will not serve this end.

Narratives launched discussions of identity, and in turn, I slipped away from the identity of academia. Students connected experiences to their own and were able to perform their narratives as discourse for understanding. By forming a storytelling club, I was able to provide an educational environment for listening to students outside of my classroom. In this club, we formed our own community. "Sharing stories and making drama are effective ways to build community within the classroom, to create a communal space where students feel safe to express opinions not yet fully formed or clearly understood and to discover the stories of their lives and of their society" (King 1993, 5). Even though we worked at the school, our community was created after school hours, a designated time for telling and sharing stories.

In 1993, one of my students, Jennifer Wooley, from East Bakersfield High School in California, who enjoyed my storytelling approach, said, "Mr. Cordi, you tell stories in all of your classes." I went on to share with her, "I know Jennifer, I stopped apologizing for this a long time ago." She interrupted, "No, Mr. Cordi, I love stories. Could we have a storytelling club at our school?" This simple exchange changed my teaching more than any other experience. I began thinking of how stories could be used in schools and built into the flow of the curriculum. I did not realize it at the time, but by forming a storytelling club, we were using story to build a community within the school. In order to be an effective teacher, one must create a community with students. It involves "creating a learning environment in [which students] . . . learn how to construct and use learning communities to expand their own learning, perspectives, and problem solving. For this to happen, we have to build foundations of trust and respect, and a willingness to engage with the learning events" (Dozier, Johnston, and Rogers 2006, 86). I informed Jennifer that I did not know how to start a club, and she, in turn, informed me she would find out. At first, we formed a storytelling club called Voices of Illusion following the same rules and guidelines for telling advocated by Sawyer. We extended learning after school with storytelling as a co-curricular place for learning and community building. Clearly, the classroom was not the only place to learn from stories. I did not have to be the person who provided the stories in order for students to learn from them. However, my students were not initially performers; they were not attached to Sawyer's storytelling structure and rules and easily made changes to meet their own storytelling needs. In fact, the students created their own unique storytelling community where they could tell stories simply because they wanted to tell them, not because they wanted to perform. It was a place where students learned to coach each other. It was also an emotional space to share how they felt when they did not seem to fit in with others. Most of all, it was a place to hear student voices.

Through the storytelling clubs, I discovered a new understanding of storytelling and recognized student learning must include oral learning. Students needed to have a safe environment to discuss and question. This idea parallels Cureton (1984), who focused on inner-city students and said students need oral learning. Often, students would share stories even though they were not on the list of tellers. They would say that someone else's story reminded them of a story they had to share. Indeed, they had to share the stories, and we always made a space for them to do so. Cureton (1984) says, "The inner city's student learning depends on oral development. The student needs to talk out, with a group, the rationale for a particular choice. This oral exchange of reasons and answers also helps to provide the lens apt student with strategies for selecting answers. Most "individualized" programs cannot provide this kind of support" (106).

My students were interviewed for a book, and they were asked, "What do you learn from telling stories?" When he was a sophomore at Hanford High, Ken said, "Storytelling can tell and teach many things from the use of drugs to a crazy aunt of the family. People don't really know that storytelling has the power to make someone cry of sadness or cry from laughter and Voices of Illusion (our storytelling troupe) is one of the many ways to show that power" (Norfolk 2006, 175). In Ken's comment, he speaks to the power of story, as well as the inherent strength he found in the storytelling troupe, where students could be powerful and tell their stories. As noted, almost all stories were accepted, and those that went against school rules could be challenged. Students could negotiate with me to tell the story uncensored. I still had to be the person to decide if it could be shared or not, but as we came to know each other, we respected our stories. Students like Heather and Michelle would often be there to help others through their stories. My students were caretakers of each other as tellers. It was not uncommon for students to air grievances with story (flunked a test, bad teaching, poor parent, etc.). We only asked for the title of a story in order to tell it. I often knew the subject of what they would tell, but more often than not, it was a surprise to me as to the depth it would be told.

When I was teaching in the high school classroom, I tried to establish community, but I initially spent more time teaching curriculum. It was through my storytelling club that I experienced the value of community firsthand. Unfortunately, my idea of high school teaching borrowed from what I remembered as a high school student. As Sadker and Sadker (1994) have argued,

> Many adults carry high school around with them always. It is a unique, eccentric, and insulated social system, a pressure cooker where teenagers rush from one class to another, shoved into close quarters with twenty-five or thirty others their age they may love, hate, care little about, or hardly know at all. It has its own norms, rituals, vocabulary, even its own way to tell time—not by the minute and hour, but . . . by periods . . . There is life after high school but what we do as adults is powerfully shaped by those years. (99)

Despite my best efforts to create community in the classroom, in my classes, we still answered to forty-five-minute periods ending with a loud bell. I felt an urgent pressure to teach curriculum over comprehension in this environment. Clearly, this schedule allowed little time to encourage students to collaboratively design lessons. However, my storytelling club, although sometimes directed by a performance, was often time students could simply tell their stories. It was a place where we would meet twice a week, sometimes even on weekends to share our stories. The students worked hard to create a social environment. Many of them served as officers, one of whom was in charge of making sure everyone felt comfortable during the meetings, calling those who missed and reminding them how important they were to the group and arranging games to help us know one another. This went against what Hargreaves, Earl, and Ryan (1996) call "a culture of individualism."

> Secondary schools may suffer from a *culture of individualism* . . . They are places where teachers own the classroom and students move around the school like passengers in a crowded airport . . . The lack of home or collective responsibility leads to a weak sense of institutional pride . . . [Secondary schools] are a "curiously fragmented experience" for students; of school bells sounding every forty minutes or to signal a changing of the guard. Isolation is still the norm for secondary students' experience . . . And the world in which they are isolated can be a large, complex, and intimidating one. This is particularly disturbing for young adolescent students whose needs for care, security, and group attachment . . . are exceptionally strong at this stage of development. (31, emphasis in original).

Students often feel voiceless in school. This was not true in our storytelling club. In fact, one of my students shared with me how insignificant she felt before she went to a festival, but this changed when she arrived. We raised $14,000 to send nine members of our troupe to Kansas City, Missouri, to perform at the National Storytelling Conference. When one member returned, she confided in me she had been scared. She said she kept asking herself what she had to offer hundreds of professional storytellers. She also shared upon returning she had never felt more powerful because many of the tellers asked for her advice. "I will never forget," she said. "It was the first time adults had listened to what I had to say."

In this place, as well as the storytelling troupe, she had a voice to engage in transformative practices, a place where, according to McCaleb (1994), "students are encouraged to develop their own voices in interaction with the voices of others and to participate in the democracy of the classroom" a place where "the teacher aims to bring out the voices of all students" (13). As Giroux (1989) notes, present schooling in America can be highly oppressive. However, when students are provided a voice to tell their own stories, they can transform: "When human beings are presented with the possibility of writing (or telling) about their world in the way they see it and describe their experiences as they live them, they become more involved in their own learning and are better equipped to transform their own lives" (McCaleb 1994, 49).

I remember when sophomore student Angel came into my classroom. She shared how her Cherokee grandmother raised her. She told us about all her mishaps, some of them criminal, and that her grandmother did not know most of it. She told unabashed story after story about being caught by the police, kicked out of school, and brandishing a knife against another student. She did not tell this simply to recount, but to speak to it as though it was a past event she did not want to repeat. She used story to talk about how hard she was working to change her life. Where in the classroom do we account for these stories?

I remember the day Shannon came into the storytelling club after school. In her hand was a small, well-worn journal. As she handed it to me, I looked up to see several of her family members standing beside her. She said, "Mr. Cordi, we would like you to help us tell my great uncle's story. His name was Chief Dan George." I was holding the collected, unpublished writings of Chief Dan George, a gifted actor and chief of the Tsleil-waututh Nation in Burrard Inlet, British Columbia. He first came to prominence in a supporting role as the native who adopts Dustin Hoffman in Arthur Penn's *Little Big Man* (1970) for which he received an Academy Award nomination. Shannon shared he had died, and her family was not asking me to edit or correct his story, but to help them tell his story. I need to understand this required more than being a teacher; I needed to be a listener. I needed to address this and not try to teach ideas, but instead, show how her uncle's life story can best be shared. As Rehak (1996), remarks, "I work with students who are so thin I can wrap my thumb and index finger around their shoulders . . . These are twelve and thirteen-year-old children. Children who should be eating constantly, moving constantly, and thinking constantly. Are they supposed to shut up and listen? Am I supposed to talk about nouns and verbs in the abstract?" (282). The knowledge they sought was not found in classrooms. The classrooms serve different purposes as Edwards and Mercer (1987) discerned:

> Schools serve many social and cultural purposes . . . but their institutional raison d'etre is always their function of passing on a part of the accumulated knowledge of a society and evaluating students' success in acquiring their knowledge. . . . But it consists of much more than given "facts"; it includes ways of operating in the world, and of making judgments . . . The boundaries of educational knowledge are continuously marked out, and reinforced, in classroom discourse. (2–3)

My storytelling club had fewer restrictions than the standard classroom. It was a place where Shannon and her family were not asking me to perform Chief Dan George's story but help them preserve it, a place where Angel could use story to heal. However, the story needed to be heard. Once spoken, it would be performed.

In terms of an interpretive frame, verbal art may be culturally defined as varying in intensity as well as range. We are not speaking here of the relative quality of a performance—good performance versus bad performance—but the degree of intensity with which the performance frame operates in a particular range of culturally defined ways of speaking (Bauman, and Sherzer 1975, 197).

We were not concerned with performance, but that the story serve a greater purpose, honoring Chief Dan George by continuing to share his story. Performance gave Shannon the power to tell her uncle's story. Shannon, who struggled in school and attended rarely, found new language through story. As Goldblatt (1995) underscores, "to ask students from marginalized communities to take on academic discourse as their own is to invite them into a world where they have no power, requiring that they check their former badges of power at the door" (27). Our storytelling group did not have an agenda; all stories were welcomed. Shannon felt powerful enough to bring her story to our community. As a teacher, I learned teaching is about creating a space for students to be heard. Sometimes, teaching does not only occur in the classroom. It is important to build a relationship with students to allow them to exercise power by being able to share what they need or what is on their minds. Shannon did not feel comfortable in a classroom, but in a place where students could tell their stories, she felt welcome to be involved. Students exercised power when they served as caretakers for other students' stories. Trust is a form of power.

I remember Mila, a student with Down syndrome, would tell a fifteen- to twenty-minute story without an ending. It was always the same topic—wanting a boyfriend. My students would quietly listen to her story and even offer tips on how to improve it. Mila was motivated to change and realized if she did not shorten her stories and find a way to end them, she would not hear other students' stories. It was not overt coaching, but it was her internal need to listen to more stories that helped her realize she needed to edit her own work. She also slowly changed the topic of her stories after hearing folktales and other personal tales from her peers. She actively listened to the stories of other students and took risks in her own telling.

I often would assist or pair up students to hear each other or provide direct coaching. The storytelling troupe needed adult intervention, but not in the same way I was a classroom teacher. As a classroom teacher, I planned lessons and taught them. As a storytelling coach, I made every effort to create a storytelling community, a place where all students could share their stories and have a place to discuss them if they desired. I also was a guardian of the teller. The one and hard fast rule I had was, "No one will make anyone feel uncomfortable." I may have been lax on other rules, but this I was not. All a student (or teacher) had to say was, "I am uncomfortable right now," and I immediately would work to bring back the comfort. My students knew this, and I think this is why countless students told their stories when they would not speak up in other classes. As Vygotsky (1978) advocates, it is important to mediate the learning of students. As Goodman (1989) argues,

> The notion that children do not need conscious, adult intervention regarding social values and social interaction stems for the sentimental and problematic assumption that children will (if only left alone) "naturally" become concerned with the well-being of others and world around them . . . Children in our schools must come to understand the way in which life on this planet is interconnected and interdependent, and that in caring for others we are in fact caring for ourselves. (109)

Performing a story can involve risk. As Elin Diamond (1996) asserts, "as soon as performativity comes to rest on a performance, questions of embodiment, of social relations, of ideological interpellations, of emotional and political effects, all become discussable" (4). I knew the rights to tell Dan George's story belonged to Shannon and her family. It was part of an inner circle of tales I simply did not have the storytelling rights to tell. As a story teacher, I needed to show how this story could be told, not concentrate on how I would share it. Instead, I helped the family see its political value. As Langellier and Peterson (2004) note, performing narratives focuses on doing things with words and asking what difference(s) it makes to do it? This type of performative storytelling recognizes the reflexive nature of narrative. In stories, students can refer back to past events.

Shannon and her family asked me to bring voice to her uncle's story so others could know him.

As a teacher, I needed to understand that "it is the reflexivity to storyteller and storyteller to audience, to shift consciousness to experience and experience to consciousness" (Langellier and Peterson 2004, 3). Bauman (1967) recognizes each narrative event can be designed for different purposes. Ochs and Capps (2001) say,

> Every (narrative) performance will have a unique and emergent aspect, depending on the distinctive circumstances at play within it. Events in these terms are not frozen, predetermined molds for performance but are themselves situated social accomplishments in which structures and conventions may provide precedents and guidelines for the range of alternatives possible, but the possibilities, the competencies and goals of the participants, and the emergent unfolding of the event make for variability. (60)

In examining these conversational narratives, according to Shuman, (1986), one must look not only at the text, but also at the relationship in the conversations: "Conversational narrative demands that we focus on content as well as on text, and on the relationship between narrative and event—not as a matter of preferentiality but as a matter of relationship between speakers and listeners and, correspondingly, between the story world and the storytelling situation" (193). The relationship narratives have in the classroom was different than in our storytelling group. In the classroom, narratives were often connected to curriculum, but as noted before, the narratives in the group could be connected to the students themselves. They needed to tell their stories. As Ochs and Capps (2001) note, "In this fashion, narratives become organized by the contexts in which they are constructed" (188). However, they could also be connected to learning from a thematic structure.

I think the most effective way to illustrate this is by reflecting upon the many thematic shows my storytelling troupe created, designed, performed, and even recorded in a professional studio.

Students spent between one hundred and one thousand hours practicing and creating storytelling shows based on themes. Some titles included "American Choices, American Voices: American History Told by Teenagers," "Non-Violent Means Told by Teens," and "Tell Someone: Keep Kids off Drugs" for elementary students. We then performed more than fifty shows yearly before recording them. However, the storymaking process also provided teaching for the students. For example, I remember how in preparing a performance for an American history program, Dawn, then a freshman, wanted to tell the story of Sojourner Truth, but instead found a book on Maria Mitchell, the first woman astronomer. I watched how she slowly found a new discovery in Maria's work as we researched to tell her story. In deciding to use this story, we had many conversations on the narrative she wanted to tell and why she would want to choose one over the other. These conversations in the making of story that really prove to teach. They told what they knew, but we also spent time searching for the untold stories. These types of stories should be in the curriculum.

However, not all the practices were without incident. I remember how a violent outburst broke out when we were creating a program on nonviolent stories. A student threw a pencil, and it hit close to the eye of another student. We talked about the issue of nonviolence as we made this program. I used this time to teach the students violence was an issue that would show up when you least expect it, but having a choice of nonviolence may help one to be less angry. It was this discussion that helped build more effective understanding about nonviolent choices. This is not to devalue the teaching that comes from performance, even the improvisational times that occur after the performance. As a teacher, it is important to value the making of story and to remember that not all stories have to be performed to be used for teaching students.

Examining my storytelling troupes for the past eleven years and what I can learn from them to improve my teaching, I have identified the following points:

- The narratives were performed in nonperformance venues, and teaching was still involved. In other words, a polished outcome of a highly performed story was not necessary.
- Many of the stories were improvisational and the making of the stories was emphasized if not more than the storytelling.
- The speech events of the story exchange changed as the narratives shifted from performance to living narratives.
- All events are possible teaching moments, not just performative events.
- Tellership was high when we shared in a collaborative method.
- Tellability was also high when we listened to students' ideas as they composed their stories.
- The narratives my students and I told were embedded in other narratives (including dominant narratives, each other's narratives, teacher narratives, etc.) because we listened to all stories.
- We were able to promote a sociocultural context of learning since we learned from each other.

Most of all, when I used story to build my curriculum, I did not realize the importance of listening to my students' stories outside of curricular needs. My storytelling troupe showed me the value of a community of listeners and tellers. I transferred this into my classroom. When I moved and began teaching in California, one student's request for a storytelling club changed my thinking. From that day forward, I was a new teacher. Only by reflecting about these changes will I improve my practice. As Mattingly (1991) informs, "Storytelling and story analysis can facilitate a kind of reflecting that is often difficult to do, a consideration of those ordinarily tacit constructs that guide practice. Stories point towards deep beliefs and assumptions that people often cannot tell in propositional ways or denotive form, the 'personal theories' and deeply held images that guide their actions" (236).

I have tried to dig deep into my personal teaching decisions using story. This reflection has helped me evaluate those choices, and the next chapter will explore these teaching changes in a different context—teaching using story and process drama. However, but, as Jones (2008) notes, "like all stories, my account is partial, fragmented, and situated in the text and contexts of my own learning, interpretations, and practices" (224). There is still more to explore. In this chapter, I detailed how after reading *Holes* by Louis Sachar my Opportunity students did not fully appreciate the difficulty involved when digging holes until they experienced it firsthand. Throughout this chapter, and in my teaching and work with stories like my Opportunity students, I needed to experience the holes in order to see them and in many cases make them significant to my own learning and teaching practice. I needed to see that by concentrating on the told stories, I overlooked the educational value in storymaking. For example, when we worked to make *The Chicken Soup for the Teenage Soul* video and were confined to the words of the text, were there other ways I could have involved my students to create and tell their stories and not the ones from the book? While the subject centered on the lives of teenagers, the time to make the stories was not provided. I also explored my understanding of how storymaking invites learning. Unlike organized storytelling, where the story performance is the experience, in storymaking, students can interrupt, offer counterstories (Nelson 2001), and, together, experience the roof with a runaway student to question and learn more about runaways. We can collect ghost stories and trouble the authenticity of the tales discovered. The standard classroom curriculum does not traditionally invite student input into its design. Student voices are often missing. Students like Lacy and Maggie have felt voiceless, and only when invited to share, felt empowered to tell their stories. They told about their lives, and the standardized classroom does not ask them to do so. In turn, Opportunity students resisted the stereotypical, master narratives (Nelson 2001) labeling them as "at-risk," criminal, or juvies and instead began to share with me their life stories, which were vastly different than the media's perceptions.

However, when students are engaged in storymaking within the fictional world, like when we experienced imaginary yet possible stories of a real runaway's journal, it was then my Opportunity students shared their own stories of wanting to run away or running away. They revealed what it was like to be labeled as outcasts. This imaginary journey or storymaking forged real connections for students to reveal their own "storied lives" (Clandinin and Connelly 1990). Within the possible world of this runaway, they told their stories. This experience helped me value what my students had to offer, their stories and the learning that occurred as a result of telling them. However, when students need to tell stories, they do, and as educators, we can participate by listening, sharing, and even making stories together providing a safe place to do so. Students need a place to tell their life accounts. We sometimes need to listen without judgment. Sometimes, as with my Opportunity students, teachers need to suspend moral declarations allowing students to use frank language. Clearly, students need community spaces to tell and share stories. When space is not provided within the classroom, students create their own community. As noted, in my school at a student's request, we started a storytelling club. Students came not to perform, but to share their lives and the imaginative worlds they created, but most of all, to share the experience with their peers. With no formal agenda, we heard Angel's story of self-mutilation, and that of Mila, who, although she had Down Syndrome, and other staff members of the school questioned if she could tell, shared a story every week about her life.

As I write, I, too, am trying to determine how I used and can best employ stories to teach my students. Story does not have to work alone; drama and story can work in concert as I uncover effective ways to teach and provide authenticity for student voices.

As I close this chapter, I cannot close upon my reflections. Instead, I open them more, not as fragmented pieces, but as integrated, multivoiced ongoing and developing understandings.

CHAPTER SIX

STORY IN CONNECTION WITH DRAMA

In the previous chapter, I struggled to understand what it meant to be both a professional storyteller and a classroom teacher. I used critical and reflective writing to explore my research questions. I privileged telling told stories as a way for students to learn. I also showed how I realized that the storymaking process could be as significant to student learning as telling stories alone. I addressed how my identity as a storytelling teacher has changed since I have explored the following: how being raised by stories has provided a foundation of how I view using stories; how my practice as a professional storyteller has blurred, causing me to question how I use stories in the classroom; how my preference for told stories in the classroom and not storymaking altered my work as a classroom teacher; and, last, how forming a storytelling club provided space for students to share, tell, and make stories. In this chapter, I continue to redefine how stories are used in the classroom using the pedagogy of process drama. I examine new ways of looking at storymaking and story performance by employing dramatic conventions. In the previous chapter, I employ improvisation when sharing stories like the stories that were developed from the runaway student's journal. I also shifted from performance to storymaking with my students, and in this chapter, I continue to do this while creating an imaginary story world together. I also detail how collaboratively I use improvisation to create story worlds (O'Neill 1995).

I continue to explore questions as I critically reflect upon my experiences with the pedagogies of process drama and dramatic inquiry. In this chapter, I will address the following questions:

1. How do I foreground the storymaking process as much as storytelling?

   In order to address this, I must include storymaking in my storytelling identity and explore how process drama and dramatic inquiry use it to help students learn from this pedagogy. I reflect as a student in this process. I also explain how I used storymaking when I was the teacher and professor of process drama.

2. How do I incorporate the audience into the learning?

   Once again, as the student, I was not part of an external audience; I was involved with other students, in some cases, my college peers, and in others, with elementary and high school students. As a storyteller, I performed for my students, in this work outlined in this chapter; performance is redefined to include how performance helps accentuate the stories used in process drama and dramatic inquiry. Aligning my understanding of how stories are used in my storytelling with how they are used in process drama allows me to dig deeper into the educational value of storytelling and storymaking. This chapter explores new dimensions of narrative and how performing changes the stories when one is not performing for an audience.

3. When students are engaged in the storymaking process, where does storytelling happen?

   In the previous chapter, I discussed the fact that I was pleasantly surprised at the amount of storytelling that happened during the informal times in the classroom. When my students were engaged in conversation, we often shared many stories. Here again, in this chapter, I outline the stories that happen as they are created using process drama and dramatic inquiry. Understanding this process assists me in creating teaching opportunities from these unplanned stories.

4. Can there be more than one teller in both storytelling and storymaking?

   In the previous chapter, I explained the value of storytelling starting with tandem telling (two tellers at one time) and moving toward improvisational storytelling. This chapter outlines stories that are primarily built by improvisation choices of my students. Using process drama and dramatic inquiry, I explain how whole classrooms are involved in the telling and making of stories.

In order to address these questions, I not only use my experience with stories to help inform my writing, but also initially I hold still the essential elements of storytelling, that is, the tale, teller, and audience. I examine how these elements change when used with process drama and dramatic inquiry.

As mentioned in the previous chapter, I examine both the text as story and the "living narratives" (Ochs and Capps 2001) and how students use conversational narratives. Stories in process drama serve both functions. Students working with teachers can create narratives such as one about traveling, but the narratives are not seen as a polished, told story. Instead, as O'Neill (1982) and Heathcote (1991) state, the narratives are episodic. They occur across a continuum within the drama. They do not follow a chronological order. The text is ever shifting and negotiated based on the facilitation of the teacher.

Other types of narratives are "living narratives." However, within process drama these narrative conversations do not necessarily occur in the past, such as, "A long time ago, this happened . . ." Instead, the students are "living through" the many stories presented in the drama world. There are also narratives that occur in the classroom that build from the fictional narratives. The teacher can facilitate using narratives to discuss and question what is occurring in the fictional world. One of the critical differences between the told stories found in storytelling is the tale, teller, and audience are more or less fixed. These storytelling elements change and, in some cases, blend when used with process drama. The tale is not one, but many, and sometimes without closure. The tellers can be many—often the whole classroom and the listener are inside the drama world and have an external audience. Both arts serve to create narratives to be shared. How this is accomplished is sharply different.

In the seminal text *Storytelling: Art and Technique*, Baker and Greene (1977) outline the importance of tale, teller, and audience: "Storytelling, at its best, is mutual creation. Children listen and, out of the words they hear, create their own mental images; this opening of the mind's eye develops the imagination." As a performance storyteller, I typically told stories for children. I agreed with Baker and Greene "that listening can be a complete experience" (xiii). I thought this was the most effective use of storytelling because of the way students listened and talked about the storytelling or about the story or "as if" we were in the story. Strum (2000) refers to this as a "trance-like" state, a time when the story becomes part of the listener's attention. However, when I first experienced process drama in the Northwestern University classroom of professional storyteller/creative dramatics professor Rives Collins, I expanded my understanding of what it meant to be in the story.

At Northwestern University, I entered the classroom noticing the chairs and tables were scattered in small, what was later revealed to be, stations around the room. There were pictures about the Wild West covering the desks and chairs. Collins, the professor, read an article to us, not as the professor, but as someone recruiting people to walk the Oregon Trail. In role, he shared that he was looking for new travelers to go with him. As a group, also in role, we chose to travel with him. We debated what to leave and what to keep for the journey. At each station, we found out something new about our journey. Along the journey, we created our narratives. Some people shared how they ate spoiled food, and they needed to do something about the situation. We listened as Collins, as part of the community, shared how one of our members was possibly dying. We experienced his breathing quickly becoming short and his skin becoming green. We pooled our abilities. Others shared their expertise, fixing wagon wheels, cooking food, and watching for Native Americans, or being caretakers for the sick. We faced real world decisions of the time when some of us became sick and we had to decide whether to leave them.

Before I entered the room, I assumed we would be working with performance. I knew Collins as a storyteller and from my prior experience as a drama teacher; I assumed we were going to engage in some type of storytelling or theater for performance. First, I observed, the storymaking process, not storytelling, was central to this approach to drama; process drama was very different from anything I had experienced.

I had to admit, at the time, I had not witnessed or been actively involved in this type of storymaking. I asked many questions to determine how I could introduce this type of storymaking into my own classroom. At that point, I had taught for eight years (including drama), but this approach was new to me. I had learned about group and tandem telling, even storytelling based on improvisational starters, but this was different than all of these. With this process, storytelling and storymaking were not rehearsed, but experienced. I needed to know more. This was a new form of storytelling, I was left with a strong desire to learn all I could about this new method of storytelling. Was it storytelling? Could the storymaking also be storytelling? Not only was I hearing about the new form, but I was also experiencing it.

Collins developed his work based upon ideas generated from O'Neill and Lambert's (1984) text *Drama Structures*. According to O'Neill and Lambert, what is important in using process drama is the structure and not the plot of the stories within the drama.

Before Heathcote's work became known, the pattern most familiar to teachers was plot. Process drama teachers see structure as overriding plot, even when the dramatization is embedded in a time sequence such as their lesson based on "The Way West" (Bolton 1998, 42). Collins used "The Way West" drama structure to engage us not in plot, but in the experience. Drama structures are defined as a series of dramatic episodes based upon a theme that can be used for teaching. O'Neill and Lambert (1984) caution about the use of plot within this structure: "Since this theme has a kind of narrative shape provided by the 'journey,' it is important not to allow the linear development of story line to take over. If it happens, the work may become a series of incidents—'what happened next.' Instead, drama is likely to arise from moments of tension and decision, or when the settlers must face the consequences of their actions" (41). This narrative structure that was developed from tensions and decisions was what at first most confused and invited me. I was confused since this use of narrative within a dramatic structure was not to "tell the story," but instead to build upon tension, which produced other narratives. I was invited because up until this time I had never seen narratives used in this way. It was a different type of performance, and the teacher was instrumental in helping to create the structure and, consequently, building more narratives.

In this case, our structures were the ways that we could use drama to engage and enter "the Wild West." O'Neill (1982) recommends ways teachers could create a living drama from the ideas. These include providing a picture, adding content and history, meetings, and suggestions about role changes and possible settings. Using these within the drama structure, I not only thought about the drama, but I also thought about how the decisions we made in the drama world could apply to the real world. I found myself wondering about how to be collaborative with others and what about the real West. The fictional story helped me question my story. I wondered how I would react to what was happening in the fictional world. This would help me relate this to my own narratives. To cite O'Neill (1982), "In creating and reflection on this make-believe world pupils can come to understand themselves and the real world in which they live" (11).

As I experienced process drama for the first time, I wondered how stories were structured within the drama and what stories might look like within the drama.

"The Way West" was a series of dramatic events purposefully structured to encourage students' investment within a drama world. Narratives were created, discarded, extended, and manipulated to motivate and sustain student engagement. As Collins read the first article, he shared the promise of traveling west. He structured and slanted his narratives to help us affirm our choice to take the journey. However, he was not telling a story of someone walking on the trail; we, along with Collins, in role, were walking the trail together. We worked from a drama structure while in present time that created a fictional past. Moffett (1983) reasons that narratives reside in the past, while drama is always in the dramatic present. In this context, although the story of the "Way West" happened a long time ago, as we enacted the stories, they resided in the present. We acted within the stories as though they occurred as we created and suggested them. "The action of a narrative is not ongoing. It has gone on; it is reported action" (Moffet 1983, 62). According to Moffett, the action of drama is ongoing; it is what is happening now. Using process drama, one can travel to a fictional world such as a time when Bessie Coleman became the first African American pilot, but the students were not moving in the world of the past as though it were "a long time ago." Instead, the story was occurring as though it were the present. Students can also investigate possible worlds such as a trip to Mars. However, again, the action is ongoing. Our narratives of "The Way West" were not in the past; rather we were walking the trail, facing crucial decisions, discussing how to treat the injured as though it were happening to us. Did the drama actualize the story to present time? In our imagined experience, we changed the stagecoach wheels when they were broken, argued over what to bring, and suffered the hardship of the trail. The use of drama allowed us to actively create the stories we were experiencing.

In performance storytelling, I can persuade the audience to listen more intently by changing my tone or even the story's direction, but I cannot deviate from a predetermined plot. Listeners are unaware of the story's basic structure. Storytellers call performance storytelling the "theatre of the mind." In process drama, narratives are not structured simply to be heard or told but are to be enacted and experienced together. The teacher helps direct the created structures, but they are built together. Collins was not the only one structuring narratives. We each added our own stories along the way. Many of these stories were negotiated. For example, when he asked if we wanted to travel, we were given choices of what to take on the journey. As a group, we decided which ideas would be best to enact. We followed some ideas about the trail, but some were not followed. As a group, we decided to settle and each buy land but we wanted to be close to each other. During the journey, we told Collins what role we enacted. Some of us choose to be riflemen or farmers. We negotiated what supplies we would need and decided if we should and how we should approach the Native Americans or attack. As O'Neill (1982) shares, "Drama is essentially social and involves contact, communication and the negotiation of meaning" (13). Students discussed, debated, and agreed why one action might be significant and others were not. Students used both verbal and nonverbal cues to create the drama world. For example, a student could simply shake his or her head no to a request. However, the student could state, "I don't want to do this, and I am not doing it. It is dangerous." Within the drama, actions spoke as loud as words. For example, when we assessed the supplies we had collectively, I remember distinctly one person who wished not to share with us. From here, many stories surfaced because this person withheld his supplies. As we imagined why he might be so stingy, one person offered, in role, an explanation detailing a fictional, sick daughter who needed the supplies. From then on, we told this enacted story as the reason the man withheld the supplies. We negotiated the story as it happened. As Heathcote (1984) supports, "Within the safe framework of the make-believe, individuals can see their ideas and suggestions accepted and used by the group. They can learn how to influence others; how to marshal effective arguments and present them appropriately; how to put themselves in other people's shoes" (13). In imagination, we used the supplies, ran out of medicine, and searched for healing plants to substitute for the medicine. Storymaking moved us into the drama world because not only did we talk about the need for

finding plants, but we searched for them. As a professional storyteller, the narratives I use are limited by the amount of overt negotiation with an audience. In process drama, the narratives only
continue to be made when they are negotiated in an open manner.
This is because they require dramatic action—to fix a wheel, one
must fix a wheel, but one must suggest it in some manner. However, the negotiation involved in performance storytelling is much
more hidden. As a storyteller, I must try to find out what the audience needs to improve the stories. They can overtly suggest stories,
but I also need to be able to "read" them to see what they require.
I am in charge of the telling. I must look at eye contact, body posture, how they stand, and their facial expressions to help direct the
telling of stories. This makes me wonder how I can use the overt
negotiation in process drama in storytelling events?

Questions emerged from the stories in "The Way West" process
drama. In organized storytelling, there were limited ways we could
talk about the story because we relied on one telling. How often
did I disregard material about the story simply because we were
limited to the told time frame of a story? Did I regulate questions
using storytelling to build a told performance? I remember that in
my acting classes we used dramatic conventions such as "rewinding
a scene" or "creating tableau" to understand character motivation
or a plot, but here we used these conventions to watch or view our
understandings of the evolving narratives. We were able to rewind
the work and to go back to it after it was replayed. This shift created
meaning to our actions. "The potential for 'living through' drama
expands, making a cascade of possibilities if the present embraces
the past and the future, if the pain of an event was yesterday or the
implication of an event is tomorrow" (Bolton 1999, 42).

O'Neill called this the "creation manipulation of time" as it creates significant meaning to the stories used in each episode. Instead
of examining narrative or even teaching terminology, O'Neill relies
heavily on the conventions of theater to explain her form of process drama:

> It is the language of the theater that Cecily O'Neill now applies to her study of how process drama works. This is not the traditional language of climax, shape plots and sub-plots but contemporary theater language of episodes, transformation, ritual, spectatorship, alienation and fragmentation.... it is improvisation that she sees as the centre of process drama, even though she may employ depiction and scripts as part of the sequence. (Bolton 1997, 42)

Stories were changed using improvisation. Some of these were changed as a result of using dramatic conventions. For example, we used tableau to show what we were experiencing on the trail. Each person created a scene, some showing hunger, some tiredness; however, we were inside the perspective—we had experienced, in role, similar feelings and actions. We were performing our learning as insiders who wanted to understand what we were experiencing. As students on "The Way West" experience, we decided to keep a journal to help others who might walk the trail at a later time. From this replaying of our fictional lives, we constructed meaning to record for others. We did not look to an outside audience to praise or critique our work because, in this sense, performance checked our progress and confirmed our learning within the dramatic structures. It also suggested other ways to explore in the fictional world.

The stories used in process drama did not consist of only one negotiation, but of many occurring at the same time. With Collins, we were simultaneously telling and experiencing stories, and each classmate added to the dramatic experiences.

Each story presented or offered is negotiated, which changes how it is used in the drama. O'Neill and Lambert (1984) believe, "In drama, the representation of experience which each individual offers to the group is subject to the scrutiny of the rest. What is offered may be modified by others, who in turn, must modify their own contributions" (13).

Unlike professional storytellers who prepare and create stories with a clear beginning, middle, and end, Heathcote (2006) prepares stories for process drama work quite differently. "I hardly even see narrative as a journey from the front end to the back end because I think stories can begin anywhere" (Heathcote 2006, personal conversation). In "The Way West" process drama, the composition of stories was less like told stories and more like the everyday narratives identified because of the interactive nature of the narratives. They depend on teller and listener and intermix between the two. Heathcote (2006) notes, "Telling stories places the power of the form and the unfolding pattern events, firmly in the hands of the teacher" (9). Many of the stories Collins shared and those we created were simply sparks or fragments of ideas told in a narrative way. There was no story closure, but the story's significance still guided our discussions. As expected, the unfolding story fragments led to additional questions. Heathcote goes on to say, "The inner part of stories focuses upon the attitude of a persona which then causes response from others, and out of these events is brought about. It is by this kind of ordering that drama produces the opportunity to make constructs" (11). In addition to stories only appearing in the fictional time for one significant moment, I also noticed some stories were not resolved, which increased our investment in the story and drama. When Collins hinted at the possibility of poisonous snakes, we began looking for them. This subtle suggestion directed by Collins, in role, was enough to include this narrative as part of the story we enacted together. As Ochs and Capps (2001) suggest, the more one increases tellership and tellability, the more group members feel they can add to the narratives. Stories within process drama can come in many shapes and sizes; they can be overlooked, neglected, and extended.

A professional storyteller is seen as unprepared if he or she does not finish a "started" story. However, when Collins teased us with a narrative fragment, only a hint of what the West might look like, it created an interest and investment. This was a skillful teaching move using just enough of a story to invite us into the learning to question and act upon it. By withholding the narratives, we were investing in continuing the trip to seek further answers within the story we created. With each step, we discovered more of the story. For me, this was a new way to use narratives, and I decided I wished to use process drama in my own classroom. Below is a description and analysis of my experience with my drama classes.

I preplanned and read about the Oregon Trail restructuring my classrooms not only to accommodate the workstations, but also to handle groups of forty to forty-five since my drama classes were large. I wrote an advertisement calling for volunteers to walk the trail. On two separate occasions during the day, I taught my classes with this dramatic structure. Each class had a different response because of the students, freshmen to seniors, 33 percent were physically handicapped and 12 percent were classified as special needs. I had to adjust the lesson to work with students who had mobility issues (wheelchairs) and in some cases, memory delays. Both classes accepted the journey, although one class took longer on deciding what to bring. For two and a half weeks, we walked the trail.

From teaching using dramatic structures, I reflected on what was significant for me, and what I could take home to my own classroom. I became aware of how the narratives may be used for teaching. I also became acutely keen as to how my role changed from storyteller and the necessity as process drama teacher to co-construct and mediate stories.

Collins made the drama experience seem effortless because he was both well prepared and skilled. From the daily preplanning involved in sustaining the drama, I learned more about using drama structures within the classroom. I learned to rely less on the exact details in the text and more on the immediacy of my students' choices in the drama. Initially, I thought we could mirror a good bit of Collins's work and text, but the stories moved quite differently with each class. I needed to plan daily. The specific choices could not always be part of my planning, but I could explore possibilities to present for the students. There is no mention in the text or the work that we did with Collins to accommodate for special needs or to prepare to make friends with the Native Americans we encountered on the trail. When my students befriended a native, asking him to join the journey, this was a highly political move that I did not plan. It was political. Because of this, it proved to be an effective teaching experience. In the drama, we could explore how to handle travel in villages that are unfriendly to Native Americans. Our guest stayed with us for a while, but we took him and dropped him off to relatives in a distant tribe. I found working with narratives only improved as I gained experience with them. The practice helped me prepare to co-direct ideas with my students both in and out of role. In my class, I could test and retest my plans. In order to plan "the westward journey," I needed to contextualize the drama to meet the needs of our classroom. This included the physical needs of students in wheelchairs who could not enter the work stations. I made the work stations accessible by using a blanket instead of a desk. With the objects on and around the blanket, all students could equally "enter" the narrative fictional world. In addition to planning for physical accommodations, I had to find a strong enough pretext to invite students into the drama. In this case, in role, I recruited others for the trail using an advertisement as a pretext. I was not building to performance but preplanning how I could invite students into the drama and allow the students to expand their knowledge with the unfolding narratives. Every day I planned ways to use narrative and other tools (drawing, writing, tableaus, etc.) to move students forward to expand their learning. Instead of retelling the work, I needed to find ways for students to actively experience it.

As a professional storyteller, I often increased investment in a told story by speeding it up at scary times or slowing it down, highlighting the eerie nature of a setting or character and, in many ways, building the tension as it was told. Altering or withholding story, too, can increase dramatic tension within process drama. As Heathcote (1984) reminds, "Tension is not a matter of huge terrifying events such as earthquakes, mutinies, armies, and so on; it is a matter of finding a lever from within the situation which is capable of laying on pressure, in the way that sore places can develop on the skin as a result of abrasion" (34). In role with my students, I chose to add elements to the drama to increase the tension. When the students were on the wagon, a wheel broke: "Hey, what was that noise? I think there is something wrong with the wagon." This trouble created further investment. As the teacher, although I could preplan elements, as noted with process drama, many other stories surfaced as we explored, taking us in many, varied directions. This spontaneity was both welcomed and encouraged to extend student investment and learning. I had planned to teach about toxic plants. Two students, in role, ate a strange plant and fell ill. Another student quickly said he had medicine. In order to invite more involvement from all students, I aggregated the situation more by saying, "Look, the bottle is leaking. There is only enough for one person." Students had to rethink their strategies in role. I deliberately troubled the situation, forcing them into action and discussion. As expected with process drama, troubling the narrative helped to create further engagement, and as a result, even more narratives surfaced. Students traded ideas in narrative form to determine their next steps. As Bruner (1991) proposes, it may be trouble that compels people to narrate. "Trouble" is felt as dramatic tension. "Trouble is the engine of narrative and the justification for going public with a story. It is the whiff that leads us to search out the relevant or responsible constituents in the narrative, in order to convert the raw Trouble into a manageable problem that can be handled with procedural muscle" (12). Heathcote (1984) distinguishes between productive dramatic tension and conflict: "Productive tension is quite different from conflict. It is the key to deepening the exploration of motive influencing action and therefore the journey. Conflict is the shallower concept for it tends to lock people into negative repetitive responses during the interactive process and prevent more subtle exploration" (108). I found that despite my understanding of process drama, sometimes my storyteller identity was foregrounded. As a result, unnecessary, unproductive tension occurred on my part that deterred the learning.

When I told the story of the westward journey within our process experience, I turned my students into listeners as themselves, rather than as enactors of drama. After we imagined a wagon wheel had broken, I found myself trying to telling the story of how the person first learned to fix the wagon wheel. I pressed him to tell us in a told story format, what his first time was like, what he learned and who taught him. I spent more time asking this student to tell his fictional story instead of allowing him to live within the fiction. Heathcote (2006) cautions story use within process drama: "Story will perhaps help those teachers who feel more comfortable if there is a plot line to anchor the curriculum, but it is somewhat poisoned chalice in that in every take is unique. It exists to fulfill itself" (16). Since I already had a riveting westward experience with Collins, I had to fight not to slip into simply retelling the same stories. Each experience should be unique, not a retold tale. Instead of telling, with other students, he could have sketched blueprints to rebuild the stagecoach or written via Pony Express to someone for instructions for parts; the choices were endless. These teaching moves also advance the drama. The emphasis is on dramatic experiential learning, not on storytelling as ourselves outside of the drama world.

As I taught, I realized that I could be the teller or a participant in the drama, but I had to be the teacher as well. Certainly, this was hard to manage because my students could stay in the fictional drama world, but I had to constantly juggle both worlds as I made teaching choices, involving both safety and directionality. As my storytelling identity surfaced, I had to resist telling the story for the students and allow myself to experience it with them. Too often I had to fight the urge to "wrap the event" with a story and, instead, allow them to discover or explore choices for the event. My telling identity said let me bring you together and tell you how this situation was resolved. However, instead of this, I let them resolve it.

As a story coach, I worked with students so they could tell the stories that we created together in the drama world. Narratives are seen differently in the context of classroom interactions. The students' choices do not always follow my preplanned narratives. Any story told, for example, the wagon wheel tale, is always serving in relationship to what is occurring now and what has occurred in the past. In other words, each narrative is connected to what has come before it. These narratives constitute a teaching experience, not because they are told, but because students question, engage, and reflect upon them. Instead of telling stories, we "evoke" ourselves using drama (Wagner 1976, 9). Using process drama, a teacher can help students recreate the experiences they talk about or suggest and call forth to appear, so they can use their imagination to engage with the drama in the present time.

According to Wagner (1976), "Dorothy Heathcote doesn't direct drama; she evokes it. Unlike most drama teachers, she allows the students to make as many of the decisions about what the drama is going to be about as possible. She makes only those decisions that must be made if what they choose to do is to happen dramatically" (9). In this sense, I do not co-direct, I co-evoke. In "The Way West" example, I preplanned a narrative or pretext to fuel our drama engagement. In the lived-through experience of the fictional world, students evoke many narratives to create the larger drama. As we create, we debate, and finally agree what narratives we pursue and those we discard. As expected, as the larger dramatic world evolves within a series of narratives, it is affected by our interactions, students' questions, and suggestions. In my role as teacher within this drama structure, I am always mindful as to how I can involve all students in these unfolding narratives as we decide where to go next. For example, in "The Way West" drama, we created a map of places we wished to explore. As we used other tools such as writing, language, drawing, and engaging in play or, in this case, the map, they can make the narrative different than in a told story. Clearly, within process drama, students can represent their learning using a trash can lid to represent a wagon wheel. This transformation from lid to wheel invites students to move into the narratives instead of simply listening to them. Consequently, during the drama, I needed to structure spaces where students could interact and create narratives and to decide the best use of the constructions. Initially, as a teller, I thought my role was to weave drama within story, but my role was actually much greater as I took responsibility for helping students to see the worlds we shape, experiencing them critically through reflection. In order to do this, I incorporated more "what ifs" and "I wonder" into the drama. This means the fragments of story, the story behind the stories, and those selections that tease are worth developing within the drama. When brought to the foreground, they become part of the collective story.

The next time I participated in process drama at the Ohio State University, it was not using predetermined drama structures, but rather using a teaching approach called dramatic inquiry. For five years at OSU, I studied, practiced, and taught the pedagogy of dramatic inquiry by Brian Edmiston (2007), which emphasizes using drama to promote inquiry with students through collaborative ideas through educational or process drama. It incorporates teacher-in-role, student-in-role, working in a fictional world, and student-centered learning.

I began to wonder where inquiry is situated in organized storytelling. I found myself referring back to the "trancelike" state that occurs in organized storytelling. Countless times, the audience questioned while I told. When my student Dawn Escobar told a story about Maria Mitchell, the first woman astronomer, another student asked her a barrage of questions, and I was told by the librarian that books describing Mitchell's life were checked out soon after. Telling the story created a need for inquiry, but this was not always shared inquiry. Students could go to the library after a story, or they could ask internal questions and research them later. Many times, organized storytelling created shared questions and inquiries about the story. For example, I remember hearing Emmy award–winning teller Bobby Norfolk share a tale about an African American, Henry Brown, a slave who sealed himself in a wooden crate for twenty-seven hours to gain his freedom rather than remain a slave. This spurred numerous questions, and Norfolk shared more of the story as a result of the questions. Many times, a story was an entry to curriculum study. For example, in telling "Little Burnt Face," we discovered other native traditions and customs. However, the inquiry questions from the students occurred after the story, not during. In contrast, the inquiry in process drama builds from questions that arise during, as well as before and after, any imagined experience.

In the following examples, Edmiston created activities to improvise what it might be like to design a school such as the Carlisle school, where Native Americans were forced to give us their identity, or what the first African American pilot felt and why she might not have succeeded. Like Heathcote, Edmiston and Taylor (2005) turn to an inquiry-based approach to curriculum.

> Learning and teaching can be contrasted with the dominant assumption that teachers merely "deliver" the curriculum to pupils. We believe that curriculum, like life should be explored rather than delivered like a parcel . . . We view teaching as mostly facilitation and mediation of learning through inquiry and we are critical of didactic and transmission teaching methods because they have left too many disaffected pupils on the sidelines of learning. (6)

The question arises: When does the inquiry become dramatic? Edmiston (2010) states, "Inquiry becomes dramatic inquiry when children and adults dramatize the inquiry process" (14). For example, in a graduate class, Edmiston negotiated with us to agree to imagine we would design a school and as we were given a dramatic context, build the school for an unknown client, and we accepted it. We did not take a passive role but were actively planning the school's design. Our questions and our resulting actions became more complex as we wrestled with new questions that arose for us. Edmiston took on the role of someone checking on our progress in order to structure and focus our imagined task and to report back to our client. In doing so, he could extend our questions and pose new ones and deepen our explorations.

In the fictional world, Edmiston, the professor, had prepared large sheets of butcher paper that represented preblueprint sheets for us, a group of teachers, to design the best school we could. We were told money was not an issue. As we began to build, we provided reports to some official on the phone. As we immersed ourselves and debated on what we needed for the ideal school, the official's conversation and suggestions began to bother us. Edmiston, in role of the official, told us were to build a school to "Americanize" Native Americans. "We need to make sure they represent our country." Over a period of exchanges, we found out what "Americanize" meant. It meant displacing their native identities, which included stripping them of their practices, customs, language, and traditions and replacing them with American ideals. As some decided if we should build the school, others prepared to do so regardless. We struggled over what to do. We were divided. Some of us wanted to be spies, and some wanted to stop building. Later, a fellow classmate Sharon shared her personal story, when her father had been placed in a boarding school and stripped from his native ways. This only complicated our difficulty, but it helped us personalize our drama.

As we explored our questions interacting with the teacher and one another, our investment deepened. This work made me wonder about how inquiry might be used with told stories. As a storyteller, I wondered how much student curiosity I was able to create and sustain with told narratives. Are there ways to help students inquire more with narratives? In my experience as a participant within dramatic inquiry, I considered how I might use inquiry to promote both storymaking and storytelling

As was noted before, O'Neill concentrates and uses drama conventions that borrow from theater to facilitate process drama. She uses improvisation to highlight tension and discussions occurring within the drama world. Heathcote concentrates on the learning that can be developed when stepping in someone else's shoes using drama to help students engage and question in the fictional world. She employs teacher-in-role to help the teacher facilitate the drama, along with the questions and "dramatic tension" to allow for deep involvement and investment in the drama. Booth uses teacher-in-role and improvisation, but this is always to be anchored for deep investment in the characters and action from a printed story. When developing process drama, Edmiston also employs improvisation, narrative, teacher-in-role, but what is highlighted is how the drama and these dramatic conventions can serve to promote sustained inquiry with the students. What is meant by sustained inquiry is that the questions created by the drama become an entrance point to develop, further question, and engage in inquiry. However, the questions are not addressed after the drama, but inside the drama. The teacher serves to facilitate the inquiry using improvisation and teacher-in-role. Students, along with the teacher, engage in inquiry on a continuum of understanding. The activities in the drama are to help extend the questions and curiosities but also to enact and engage in the understanding of the questions by being in role as someone who has an investment to discover more about their questions. "Dramatic inquiry begins when adults participate in, and mediate, collaborative activities in the overlapping spaces of young people's inquires and their dramatic improvisation" (Edmiston 2010, 15). Using Heathcote's strategy of teacher-in-role, Edmiston engaged in the drama both as an official (in role) and professor in order to support and extend our curiosity of our learning through inquiry. He deliberately withheld certain information, which was a skillful way to use narrative as we built the school and as the official's stance became questionable in response to our desire to know more about why we were building the school. Each teaching move fostered our inquiry and discussion to decide how to proceed or what to do next. However, this approach was not simply asking questions; we created a fictional world where we could address and explain answers to these questions.

The *American Heritage College Dictionary* (2002) defines inquiry as "a question; a query" (716). But the inquiry that grounds the pedagogy of dramatic inquiry goes further. Participants' questions ground their deepening explorations, which they can pursue in fictional situations as well as everyday conversations. Using drama, we engage in a continued pursuit to explore the inquiry questions using role and creating a fictional world. We did not simply ask why we were building the school; we debated it with the official. We did not simply announce it is wrong to do this, but we argued as fictional teachers why it was wrong and what we were going to do about it. And most importantly, we acted upon our questions and responses. We agreed upon a moral stance.

We decided to build the school, but in a way to appreciate Native Americans and not deny their culture. In our interaction with the teacher-in-role, we defended our choices. All in all, we sustained our inquiry by working from a continuum using drama, questions, and activities in the fictional world.

Richard Beach and Jamie Myers in their text, *Inquiry-Based English Instruction* (2001), introduced six inquiry strategies to help organize inquiry: immersing, identifying, contextualizing, representing, critiquing, and transforming. This helps the inquiry become dramatic with drama and story. Students can step into the trouble and even attempt to fix and evaluate in and out of role. I provide an example.

Using drama, all the strategies were presented as we created and then questioned the world we created. In the building of a school drama, we entered the world of building a school to "Americanize" the students. We immersed ourselves in the world we were presented. However, along the way, we had concerns and identified that it was not simply building a school, but if it was right to build this school. We contextualized our roles as teachers, but also human beings, and we critiqued our choices to serve in these roles. By the end of the boarding school drama, after hearing Sharon's story of her father, some people were transformed by the experience. I was one of them.

In storytelling, we can immerse ourselves in an imagined social world. Students can engage in a storylike trance as they follow the storyteller, for example, as he or she takes a trip through the eyes of a Civil War soldier, Brer Rabbit trying to get out of tar, or a giant trying to catch Jack, who has his golden goose. Stories, too, can identify problems or issues such as fighting a war against your brother, not knowing how to get out of a sticky mess, or running fast enough to get away from a giant. The storyteller also creates the context, and the listener chooses whether to buy into it. The storyteller lets us wander as a soldier, hear Brer Rabbit talk, and run with Jack. A storyteller can also position one soldier over another and create a critical perspective on war. He or she can show the danger of not treating everyone fairly by using Brer Rabbit as a metaphor for accepting differences and can show how Jack feels bad when he hears of the giant dying from falling off the beanstalk. It is the last strategy, transforming, where dramatic inquiry stands out. Storytelling by itself does not examine the path not taken, even though it is implicit in the story. Instead, the storyteller directs the listeners on the path of the story. Storytelling does not allow for this kind of revision except through enlightenment. Sometimes a story will be powerful enough to produce change. Transformation is a powerful teaching tool, and as a teacher, I need to use dramatic inquiry with stories if I want my students to really rethink the choices in the story.

"The primary purpose of engaging in inquiry is to help students to gain an understanding of how we construct or author the social worlds we inhabit" (Beach 2001 20). Using dramatic inquiry, students can not only understand their own social worlds, but they can imagine other people's social worlds as well. Using tools such as butcher paper to design and represent what "schooling" means to them, helps students be transformed. They transformed because these tools helped them experience discomfort and change as they engaged in the drama. In organized storytelling, as noted, transformation can occur as a result of being enlightened to change. I think of Patty Larkin's story song, "Metal Drums," which tells the story of children playing in nuclear plants. They die early from cancer. This one-story song transformed my understanding of the danger of nuclear plants. Other stories such as the ones often told by the trickster Mullah Nasrudin offer simple wisdom by showing the folly of actions. In a story where Nasrudin loses his keys, he only searches in a well-lit area even though he lost them in the dark of the room. This simple story helped guide me to look where things are lost and not where they are easy. Narratives in dramatic inquiry can occur because socially the stories not only are told, but also are shared, challenged, and evaluated by the class and teacher. How as a storyteller can I create this experience?

Lakota and Plains Apache teller Dovie Thomason told one story that closely resembles the one we created in our graduate class at a storytelling festival. She shared a personal tale of how the Carlisle boarding school stripped away her grandmother's identity. The story moved me; it brought back this experience and a recent experience when I worked with San Juan Pueblo Estafaez Martinez, also known as "Blue Water." I spent two days with her listening to her stories of the San Juan Pueblo and then hearing her tell the sad account of growing up in a boarding school. When recalling these stories, I am able to remember other narratives as well and be transformed because they are powerful. As every storyteller soon realizes, stories create other stories. When listeners are in the storytelling trance, they often refer to narratives that have occurred to them while the story is being told. It is almost expected that a handful of listeners will tell you stories based on the story you told. This is part of the storytelling connection. Thomason's story brought me back. As I plan for stories to be told, I also should plan for the stories that occur from them. They too can be used for learning.

As a storyteller, when I shared tales with my students or even when they created their own, a sense of closure was key. Closure amplified the learning through the full story cycle of beginning, middle, and end. However, using drama, we were able to share the real account of Shannon's father, but even with this story, it did not close the drama experience for me. My reaction to this continued to trouble me after the class.

In the fictional world of story—the story of the school—we made real choices. Our inquiry enhanced learning and created understanding: "People dramatize inquiry not through performance for an external audience, but by imaginatively and collectively projecting into the socially imagined spaces of a fictional world where they can enact possible events to better understand something" (Edmiston 2010, 15). As in life, some stories are not resolved. I remember, as a class, we wondered if we should quit building the school, but when we were informed others would build it regardless, we decided to explore becoming covert spies in order to sabotage the project, all the while still remaining in the imagined group of designers. Even as we struggled with our choices and decisions, we never resolved our problems. This experience allowed me to reflect upon how I used stories in the classroom. I privileged my curriculum as a storytelling teacher and provided spaces to finish stories. I helped students when creating stories to work to possible conclusions emphasizing the ending as a viable part of both the storymaking and the storytelling. Withholding information can create educational discomfort. In other words, in the fictional world, the teacher can deliberately create conflict to extend classroom learning. My background as a storyteller, from the time I was raised with tales of Appalachia to performing on a stage, I was told, and even judged, on closing my stories. The tales my mother told me on the couch always had closure. Jack always had an ending, often returning to his mother to start a later tale. With dramatic inquiry, the goal was not resolution, but advancing learning through extended inquiry.

The boarding school narrative we created had no resolution. I hoped for a happy ending that never came. What happens when an ending is not sharp or clear? Drama, especially unresolved drama, can allow us to connect and extend learning about a fictional situation with personal understanding. I know I was troubled with the school drama because shortly before this experience, when I traveled to tell stories in New Mexico, I had spent three days with "National Treasure" storyteller Blue Water from the San Juan Pueblos. Although she shared she was a product of a boarding school, I did not fully understand what this meant until this drama experience. As I was involved in the drama, I continued to reflect upon her story, blurring the personal with the fictional. I wanted a happy ending; I wanted Blue Water to come out okay.

The impact from this experience was not short-lived. In fact, I remember e-mailing Edmiston explaining how the results of our unresolved stories haunted me. I asked him how I could conclude the drama, for even though it was long over, it was still in my head. He assured me leaving it unresolved was intentional because when drama leaves you wondering, it invites you to explore more. This convinced me how essential the teacher's role is within dramatic inquiry. While the teacher uses drama to help students learn, he or she must also recognize when the story is too personal. During the work, Sharon shared her father's story. At one point, she did not feel ready, and Edmiston gave her full permission not to tell. His mediation provided a space for her to tell if she wished to do so. In organized storytelling, as noted, we could not ask questions until the story concluded. In contrast, using the pedagogy of dramatic inquiry allowed us to pose questions and act upon them together, creating the stories we imagined.

As a class, we debated how and if we should construct the school. We heard a personal narrative from one of our fellow students, and we talked in role. The stories were shared, debated, contested, and negotiated. Stories were not the only tools used to mediate the drama. We combined writing, dramatic conventions, and other tools. In the boarding school dramatic inquiry, we used paper as school blueprints, we stood in tableau representing a sculpture to be placed in front of the school, and we created dramatic episodes showing what our school looked like by creating statues. All of these were tools—symbolic ways to promote our investment and focus inquiry. Wolf and Enciso (1994) say that "beyond this verbal expansion is the spread of meaning making using alternative symbolic systems—art, gesture, drama, and music as participants interpret text simultaneously through multiple channels" (352–53). This experience made me reflect more upon how tools may be used in storytelling. In organized storytelling, storytellers often only use language and their bodies as tools for telling. In fact, instead of viewing drawing, music (some do, some do not), and writing as something that accessorizes the story, when we are working in classrooms, we need to be open to how we can use other tools to help children learn with story. As a storyteller, I can hopefully find ways to use tools in performance as well as the storymaking process in classrooms. I need to find ways to expand on how I include and use tools, not only in my use of process drama but also in my storytelling work so that all students are involved in the learning process.

Heathcote supports when using story as a process of making meaning, it is not used for creating something like a performance, but instead becomes a tool for creating narratives and promoting learning. When asked what process drama does not include, her answer was a play or story for acting out and explaining a story. Instead of explaining with story, the emphasis is on experiencing stories (Heathcote 2006).

There is not a story so much as an episode in which possibilities can emerge. These episodes are very focused to serve the needs of the participants: talking responding, thinking, using previous experience, consulting, finding out by doing, trial and error, and considering (Heathcote 2006, 9).

In examining the narratives used in the boarding school dramatic inquiry experience, Edmiston interrupted the narrative to either present new ideas or question our actions in both the fictional and real world. Breaking the story as Edmiston did to present or demonstrate is not generally done with organized storytelling, but here it served as an effective teaching move to help us engage more deeply in our inquiry. For example, when we were discussing and building the statue for the front of the school, Edmiston broke into the story, asking how the arms would appear. He demonstrated by showing how they would reach out as though they were welcoming. His breaking of the story invited us to wonder more about what we were saying with the statues. Interrupting the story is an effective move in process drama (Bowell and Heap 2001).

> We would all agree, we are sure, that drama could be described as stories in action. This might lead us to suppose that events in drama have to unfold in a chronological order. However, this is certainly not the case, just as it is not always the case in stories, and in fact if we do always stick to a mono-directional time sequence we will miss a great opportunity to construct a tight and engaging drama and restrict the pupils' opportunity to explore the issues of the drama in as full a manner as might otherwise be possible. (96)

With process drama, one effective teaching move is the skillful placement and organization of narratives. Using dramatic inquiry can focus students on being critical about what they experience in the drama world as well.

Working in an arts-magnet, urban school in a fourth-grade classroom consisting of African American and European American children, my colleagues and I used drama to step into the world of Bessie Coleman, the first African American pilot. Students imagined they were with her when Edmiston blocked her attempts to be a pilot. Taking on the role of a white owner of a flight school in the 1920s, the students, also in role, stood in a single line and walked past another student in the role of Bessie Coleman and said the obstacles that might keep her from being a pilot. A number of students said money or status, but I vividly remember one white student saying quietly, "Because you are black." The student, in response to the teacher's questioning, provided a critical doorway in using drama to discuss the sensitive issue of race. When the young, white child opened the door into the fictional world, he focused on race and social justice.

If, as teachers, we want to teach for social justice, I propose that we need to make power relationships more visible as we build nurturing, collaborative, and fair communities in our classrooms. We cannot teach about social justice in the world outside of the classroom if we do not run classrooms based on what social justice means to children on a daily basis: fairness, caring, and sharing. We can use drama toward these aims (Edmiston and Bigler-McCarthy 2006, 2).

When teaching for social justice using drama, students do not simply address issues; they enact them. Teachers can introduce drama to both change and demonstrate power relationships. When Edmiston was in role as a white, racist flight school owner, the students, both black and white, addressed the owner using drama. In the fictional world, they can in role explain why it is wrong to treat others this way. Edmiston, in role, positioned himself as someone who was not kind. As Edmiston (2009) informs,

> Social situations and relationships may change radically when children play (or are engaged in process drama). Teachers using dramatic inquiry may shape social interactions to change the power relationships among children and adults. In play, existing relationships become destabilized, and through dramatic inquiry more complex relationships may develop, as imagined communities begin to grow in classrooms. (20)

In this drama, I was working with a fourth grader who was African American, and Edmiston had asked the students to draw an event in the story. This student drew a plane with a bomb attached to it to explain a possible reason why Bessie Coleman's plane had crashed. This drawing became a mediating tool to launch an additional discussion on the events surrounding the crash. No cause was ever determined for the plane crashing, so it was possible a bomb caused the crash. I began to talk about this from the fictional world that we enacted and from the real world as to why she thought this way. We were able to discuss drawing from her experience, in which she shared how white people can be mean, and the experience of the fictional world of Bessie Coleman demonstrated how some white people react to black people. The drama and the drawings were mediating tools to engage conversation of how people are treated differently because of the color of their skin. It was not planned out. It happened as a result of the drama; I improvised with the student and the other students. The improvisation using these tools also served to help students learn using drama.

According to Heathcote (1991), improvisation is the process of "discovering by trial, error and testing; using available materials with respect for their nature and being guided by this appreciation of their potential" (44). The product of improvisation is the experience. Viewing these narrative experiences as a collection of episodes, I recognize that each episode creates possibilities for learning. A child's saying, "Because you are black!" was not planned out but arrived only after a series of improvisational choices with students, which included taking a racist tone as a white flight instructor, using flashback to imagine a white washer woman's reactions to Bessie when she was a child, to physically standing in a line as a fictional Bessie Coleman tried to advance through the line. Through improvisation within the fictional world, students reacted and even debated racism. Holland (1998), taking a cultural anthropologist view, argues that people act through the play in improvisation. As students play in dramatic inquiry, "Children are free to improvise actions and responses within the implicit social rules of imagined situations" (Vygotsky, 1976). Change the imagined scenario, and you change the social rules and thus the possibilities for action and making meaning using whatever cultural tools are available and appropriate in the new situation (Edmiston 2010, 23).

Edmiston introduced an environment where racism could be both enacted and questioned within the drama. Teachers can use improvisation and mediating tools to make social justice issues more visible. Students, with the help of the teacher, can decide how to move through the drama. By changing the point of view when telling the story of Bessie Coleman to a racist, white, flight owner, more narratives and possibilities surfaced. As a storyteller and a teacher who uses stories, I explored the significant times I engaged in inquiry, using mediating tools. Basically, "fictionalizing an activity alters how people relate to one another" (Edmiston 2010, 19). Now it was my turn to teach using process drama, highlighting inquiry and narratives in the drama. This experience showed me how drama can motivate what others might consider the reluctant student.

Another graduate student, Chad, and I were invited to a history class where we planned to teach a lesson about a small village in England known as Eyam. In this fictional town, many of the residents sacrificed their lives so others in nearby villages would not be affected by the rampant spread of the Black Plague. Starting with a personal story of my trip to Eyam, we used this experience to imagine ourselves as members of the town and participants in the town meeting—the same town meeting where it was decided whether people should sacrifice their lives. Students became townspeople, and I became the village mayor.

Some students are quiet, reserved, or content not to be involved in most classroom activities, what Edmiston (2008b) calls students on the edge of learning. Stories used in drama can reach these students and draw them into the work. After I had completed this drama, I was told a student on the edge of learning was in the class. Neither Chad nor I could tell based on how involved and invested the student had been in the drama. At the town meeting, we discussed which residents we could afford to lose in the town because they already had signs of the disease. Students nominated people and talked about why they could/should be left to die.

The normally quiet student was so incensed he used his role to exclaim, "How could we be so damn careless with people's lives?" He explained that he was the blacksmith, and even if he had the disease, he would still be the blacksmith. He screamed, "Who were we to play God?"

The world of the classroom kept this student quiet, but the world of drama, as an active participant in the unfolding story of the Black Plague, released his voice. Edmiston (2010) says, "Dramatic inquiry can be extremely significant way of organizing learning providing children with ways to access and create new ways to think and communicate about the world that just could not be available in the classroom" (21). This student who was considered an outsider in learning stepped inside the fictional world to discuss real issues such as the value of human life. Edmiston goes on to say, "In dramatic inquiry, when students take dramatic action (as if they are in an imagined time-space) they can experience significant events in the lives of characters from books or other narratives, represent those events, and then reflect upon such imagined moments in order to evaluate deeds in the lives of those people." The student was moved by the drama to respond. Edmiston continues, "Additionally, it is when people interpret such imagined events metaphorically (rather than literally), (they) make connections with their own life situations" (9). Working within the fictional world allows students who might be considered to be displaced to have a voice. This voice allowed this student to speak out, but also other students in role to speak back. They engaged in imagined yet real conversations such as how many others would be infected if certain people did not leave the community. What was the value of one person over another? This was a spirited exchange and not simply a speech. This imagined heightened dialogue led to real conversations about the value of life.

The teacher and I and, later, Edmiston worked with four second-grade urban children who were blind. One student also had cerebral palsy. They were interested in exploring Mars, and for four weeks, we used drama to create a mission to Mars. From this experience, I saw how students could step into the roles they could not necessarily hold in their real lives. In other dialogic inquiry experiences, I had seen students step into the roles of German children during the Berlin Airlift, African American pilots, students attending Houdini's séances, engineers on the *Titanic*. We had students who were blind see in the fictional world. With these four students, we built a spaceship and used clay models and braillers to communicate with the Martians.

When we landed, the students created a cosmic dust that clouded the adults' eyes while shielding the students and astronauts. This left us blind, so the "blind" students volunteered to lead us. In the real world, these were blind students walking into a classroom, but in the fictional world they were experienced, seeing astronauts leading their teammates who were temporarily blind around the planet Mars. It was here I saw how the use of drama provided students more than a voice to speak; it gave them a world to see. Using drama, I watched students ask questions about Mars, including its size and ability to sustain life. They wanted to know how Martians could survive. As a teacher, I was guiding or mediating their inquiry; I was not instructing them. I was later told outside of the classroom that two of the students spent their time sitting for hours listening to radio or TV. Their parents did not communicate with them besides basic needs. These same students were using drama and able to argue with me in role as Senator John Glenn to determine if they should allow international astronauts aboard their ships. They led us around when we could not see. They wrote to their fictional girlfriends /wives or boyfriends/ husbands explaining why they were leaving the planet Earth and how they would miss them. In the fictional world, being blind was not a deterrent to visiting Mars.

On the last day, the students presented a giant comic book written in both Braille and English peppered with pictures displaying the difference they had made on Mars. This was not an assignment; this was a gift to me. Clearly, they wanted to remember the experience and were empowered to create a lasting document commemorating it. Using drama, they had presence in the classroom.

Edmiston (2010) says, "Dramatic inquiry can be an extremely significant way of organizing learning when it provides children with ways to access and create new ways to think and communicate about the world that just could not be available in the classroom but which are located in aspects of life about which they desire to learn more expertise" (17). In the fictional world, those students who sometimes got dismissed because of their disabilities went to Mars! Their pride transferred to the everyday classroom.

As Edmiston (2007) notes, "Drama can productively disrupt the sense of classroom normality to create spaces where children can be viewed primarily as using their strengths in learning literacy practices, rather than children with or without disabilities" (338). These students were able to engage in the world of Mars. Despite being blind, at one point, the students in the fictional world of Mars searched for poisonous spiders, talked with John Glenn, wrote to their boy/girlfriends and experienced a rocket launch. However, we accommodated the experience not limiting their experience, using what they knew such as creating images out of Play-Doh or typing on a Brailler. These tools were used to accentuate the experience in the fictional world. Students fashioned a scale model of Mars from the clay, and the Brailler was used to speak to aliens. We learned to mediate in a world where physically they could not see, but in the fictional world they experienced all the world of Mars.

In organized storytelling, teachers do not always include students with physical and mental handicaps because they think they "can't sit through it for a long time." In this use of story, they don't sit; they create. As a teacher, I need to keep this use in mind as I work with students who have special needs.

Picture a classroom where students think as engineers on the ship *Titanic*. One student is concerned with what type of wood was used to build the ship's interior, another wonders about the iceberg's impact, and still others search for clues to explain the ship's sinking. As we expanded the drama, students were invited to become the engineers, using dramatic inquiry as we explored these issues.

The *Titanic* drama experience challenged my narrow understanding of telling a story. In dramatic inquiry, many narratives abound. It is up to the teacher and students to determine the significance of the narratives presented. The teacher can help align certain narrative using mediation (Vygotsky 1978). "The drama teacher's function (or the teacher that uses drama) . . . is not primarily to instruct pupils or to pass on any body of knowledge. The teacher is seen as attempting to create potential areas of learning in which pupils can participate" (O'Neill 1990, 21).

When a student said he argued with Captain John Smith and then remembered deliberately leaving a window open on the ship, suggesting this was the reason for the sinking, I had to mediate to move to another narrative. The learning was not about revenge or anger, but instead, about plausible reasons to determine why the ship sank. Because an open window high on the ship would not sink a large vessel, we agreed this was not a narrative to explore further. When mediating storymaking, I had to position this student to have less power in the drama. If we had engaged in his narrative, the rest of our work would have taken directions that did not move us closer to exploring the actual causes. I had to mediate the significance we gave to this story. In turn, I mediated how much power this student's story would have in our inquiry. As Edmiston continually reminds me, as a teacher one must be both in the inside (fictional world) and the outside (classroom) to make the best teaching decisions. I had to constantly ask myself, Would this help us build our understanding? And, if so, how do I share this understanding, so we can all be a part of it?

I also shifted roles to promote learning. Heathcote (1976) prefers a "middle position" (129) so students can exercise more power. Therefore, I reviewed my uses of process drama, and instead of choosing the role of the ship's captain, I became a fellow engineer alongside my students, although I could shift between roles.

When choosing a role, certain, specific guidelines apply in process drama. Heathcote (1976) suggested the following guidelines:

1. Stay in role only as needed.
2. Give information nonverbally.
3. Use the role to keep the group together.
4. Use role to evoke explanation.

To illustrate these guidelines, I use a process drama lesson that I taught about the *Titanic* where I began in role as an engineer. Later, I became the captain because I wanted the students to follow orders. In the same drama, I switched again to a member of the press corps, so I could hear them explain what might have caused the ship to sink. Each teacher-in-role move was deliberate to help students learn new information. I could change the situation both verbally and nonverbally.

As a captain, I stood tall to communicate my authority. However, I did not stand as tall as an engineer because I did not want to be seen with higher authority than the students who were in role as engineers. As a fellow engineer, I worked with students to help create a statement for the press. Teacher-in-role can lead to deeper engagement within the classroom drama. The shifting of roles (e.g., engineer, captain, press) can heighten engagement. Students might tell something more private to a fellow engineer than to a captain. As the teacher, I need to decide what role will help the students reflect best about the experience. "As different roles in different situations are undertaken, so pupils grow in their capacity to respond appropriately and effectively within the drama" (O'Neill and Lambert 1982, 141). Heathcote (1976) supports both teacher-in-role and the shifting of these roles in creative ways to use drama to reflect and extend thinking. The value is in the unpredictability of how the roles are used. Instead of defined roles, they shift and extend the learning. Captain John Smith surfaced because students wanted to hear from him. It was not preplanned; they asked how he might feel when his ship went down. The learning was extended because they asked the captain something only he could answer. As Heathcote (1984) stresses, "The most important aspect of role taking is that it is unpremeditated, unplanned and therefore constantly can surprise the individual into new awareness" (Johnson and O'Neill 1984, 51).

Students can have more power with drama than in everyday life. For example, when students wanted to talk with Captain John Smith, finding him sad, they wished to cheer him up. Because students wondered about Smith, we had him appear. While each student shared comforting words, one student told him: "God will provide." Many students laughed at this. I remember the student turning around and saying, "It is true." Her own religious story was important to her fictional role. I showed the students how important talking to the captain was and at the same time honoring the young woman's religious stance. I made a teaching decision to change the tone to honor each offering to Captain Smith. I had the students create their suggestions, but instead of saying them, they could whisper them, almost like a prayer. This way, the students understood the words were shared in sincerity.

As Edmiston (2010) states, "When adults assist, critical inquiry questions can be contextualized in engaging imagined-and-real spaces of dramatic inquiry, focused on power relationships, and explored by students in improvised activities that are both playful and performative" (3). Instead of just telling the student her religion had a place, we created a tone of dramatic reverence. Clearly, so that students honor the words offered to Smith.

Unlike organized storytelling, the tale used in dramatic inquiry can change quickly in order to support effective learning. One can switch from telling various narratives as engineers on the *Titanic*, to explaining to the press why the ship sank, to sharing bits of advice with Captain John Smith, so he can find some comfort from tragedy.

These decisions lead into the role of teacher as teller. The teacher constantly negotiates both the fictional and classroom environments, deciding what to move and how the learning can be mediated by shifting the narrative. Teachers can break the narrative introducing questions such as, If the iceberg did not hit the *Titanic* the way it did, would it affect the outcome? As much as the teacher is teller, he or she is a listener as well. Working to hear student voices so a comment like, "Because you are black" can become more significant. The teacher needs to stay connected, constantly making decisions how to use narrative as well as the other tools (writing, drawing, etc.) to promote inquiry. Dramatic inquiry creates opportunities for reflection, both fictional and personal, where students can use story to express meaning. Bruner (1994) argues narratives shape meaning; the past, living the present, and directing the future. "Life as led is inseparable from a life told—or more bluntly a life is not 'how it was' but how it is interpreted and reinterpreted, told and retold" (36).

By playing in a fictional world, students do more than just tell their stories; they interpret and reinterpret them with other students. They are able to question, trouble, and change narratives by living within them. They step into shoes they would never have a chance to choose, and once in these shoes, they experience how they fit and what it means to wear them. In exploring how stories are used in drama, like the tale, teller, and the listener, I, too, shift my understanding of teaching with story no longer working toward a told performance, but using story along with other tools to promote further learning. In the next chapter, I examine "ensemble storytelling," which is a blending of organized storytelling, process drama, and dramatic inquiry. It is a way to involve more students in the storymaking process. Additionally, I chronicle how it can be used to create improvisational performances and for creating inquiry-based curricula. These processes are new. It continues to be refined and nuanced along my life-long journey to uncover effective methods to educate using story. Whether we are storytellers, or teachers who use drama, learning should be the desired outcome. How we arrived there depends on our energy and our planning, and most of all, our willingness to let go of traditional teaching and find a new energy.

When we have had acquaintance via the storytellers, the poet, the author, and the playwright with the emotions and situations of other people, who knows what energies may be released in us for greater sensitivity, greater comprehension, new knowledge of our society and others (and even of ourselves) and of new awareness of our relationships with those near to us in the community in which we live. It is this that concerns us when we consider drama in our schools (Heathcote 2006, 10.)

Educators can create new relationships between and among storytelling, storymaking, process drama, and dramatic inquiry in order to enhance and improve their teaching, inviting curiosity and exploration within the curriculum.

CHAPTER SEVEN

NEW MIDDLE
HOW I AM EMPLOYING WHAT I KNOW ABOUT STORY AND DRAMA

Booth (2005) says, "In my work, story and drama are forever linked ... Perhaps I require the safety net of narrative in order to attempt the leap into creating stories together through drama" (8). Like Booth, I see story and drama linked, but the way they are linked was not revealed to me until I was a student of and taught process drama, dramatic inquiry, and narrative.

This analysis has resulted in a critical reflection of my work as both a storyteller and a teacher who uses stories. It is critical because it goes beyond who I am or was as a storyteller and instead looks at how stories are used in dramatic contexts using process drama and dramatic inquiry. As a storyteller, I have incorporated both storytelling and storymaking into my classroom, and as a teacher, I have discovered stories do not have to be produced to be significant to the learning and by complementing the classroom curriculum. Most importantly, I have uncovered through scholarly research, direct study, and classroom application how storytelling and storymaking can transform educational contexts extending the learning for students. This discovery informs my newly formed pedagogy, making a significant difference in how I structure my teaching.

Process drama with storytelling and storymaking as pedagogy has reshaped my teaching understandings. Before I used process drama, when I was a storyteller, a told story was the anticipated goal of my teaching. I used the storymaking process to serve the storytelling. This was part of my storytelling identity. However, this identity has shifted to include new ways to use stories with drama. When I was introduced to process drama and dramatic inquiry I experienced firsthand how the stories could complement the drama and how the drama could be used for learning. When students are involved in an imaginary, story-based world, they have new perceptions and outlooks and can actively engage in ways unavailable to them in the real world. This use of stories was not to serve the storytelling, but to serve the learning. I adjusted my teaching to respond to the fictional world we co-constructed. In the case of dramatic inquiry, stories could be used to serve a sustained inquiry—students use stories to engage and enact a fictional world where they collectively can continue their questioning. As a teacher, I build my curriculum from their questions and how they move within the fictional world to address them. This was new to me as a storyteller.

As a storyteller, I soon discovered that students needed a place to share stories. The classroom was not always conducive to sharing—students often felt silenced or disenfranchised. From a student's suggestion, we created a venue—a storytelling club—to honor student stories, providing a safe place to tell and grow in story. However, using stories and process drama showed me the classroom could accentuate student voice where students can act in role as someone else, but at the same time, collectively build curriculum. I did not anticipate how influential this experience would be in opening my eyes to alternative teaching strategies with stories. It not only changed my method of teaching, but also shifted my identity as a teacher. Identity is shaped by others (Oring 1994). I no longer worry about titles; instead, I use stories as tools to enhance learning. Students are not voiceless when everyone helps someone off a mountain, plans and travels to Mars, or tries to save others from the Black Plague. Using process drama, students can become tellers, listeners, and "doers" in the fictional world. Every choice has meaning because as the students co-construct their understandings in role, they learn other valuable skills like relating to each other, collaborating, and planning as a team. By telling their stories in roles, they also tell their own stories. They are telling how they move in the fictional world. This is a powerful teaching tool to remember as I plan to use stories. As I implement process drama to understand how stories are used, my identity as a storyteller transforms to something new. I am in the middle of being a storyteller and a teacher, and the product improves my teaching. However, in serving as the role of teacher and teller and now writer of these experiences, I am also an audience to the work. With writing, I am able to examine my work as a teacher who uses stories in diverse ways and as a teller who teaches using stories. I am an audience for my work. This reflection helps me see the new middle.

As I write this chapter, I am reminded initially how my work reflected my wrestlings as both an artist and a teacher. I drew upon Mora's (1993) idea of a "new middle," where identities intersect to form a new, enhanced understanding. This understanding has changed the way I identify and is as a result of the situational and contextual identities that have formed from tradition, experience, and questioning how these have changed in new experiences and situations.

IDENTITY

My individual identity was defined by who I was—both a storytelling artist and a practicing classroom teacher. These identities are performed as well. Each identity shaped my understanding to form my new middle. I cannot ignore, nor do I wish to neglect or abandon, these identities; rather I embrace and critically examine them to explain who I am today.

Initially, my past, being raised by Appalachian parents and later trained as a professional storyteller, helped form my personal identity. As noted by Oring (1994), when those memories shift into "discernable configurations" (212), a personal identity develops. This configuration of identities—storyteller and teacher—informs my teaching. In this study, I reveal how it became difficult to transition between the identities of teacher, storyteller, artist, drama specialist, process drama teacher, and classroom teacher. What I have recognized from Peterson and Langellier and Peterson (2004) and Bauman (1967) as a result of this study, I "perform" these identities when I need them. They are not solid or fixed, but instead, when understood can be used to improve my teaching. I have used storytelling and storymaking to perform who I am. These narrative experiences, many of them told here using methods such as autoethnography, have helped me realize who I was, who I am, and who I am becoming. In other words, I am all of these, but not always at the same time. I draw upon my storytelling identity for told stories as they relate to my identity as a dramatist and teacher. My individual identity is not shaped by itself; instead, my work with others helps form the identity I perform.

As Keller-Cohen and Dyer (2000) note, narrative is connected to identity. "In contemporary scholarship it has become commonplace to observe that speakers use the site of narratives to construct particular identities . . . the construction of identity being understood not as a single act, but as a process that is constantly active, each telling a story offering the narrator a fresh opportunity to create a particular representation of herself" (150). Using stories in process drama and dramatic inquiry required me not to operate exclusively as a storyteller or teacher, but to use role to engage and co-construct alongside students also in role within a drama world context to promote learning. I stepped away from my traditional and comfortable identities (storyteller, teacher) to discover how these new roles, both fictional and real, extended and strengthened my teaching capacity. I explored Mars as a fellow astronaut side-by-side with my students. I searched for answers as a news reporter when Bessie Coleman's plane went down. As a BBC reporter, I carried the mountain climber's stretcher asking questions in role just like my students to extend our inquiry.

As an active agent in the narrative, I, too, shaped and even directed story much differently than through performance only.

Oring (1994) notes collective identity forms as a result of experience "that produces the deep sense of identification with others" (212). Using teacher-in-role and experiencing student-in-role changed my perspectives on teaching. I was able not only to experience an "insider's perspective" but also able to see how this perspective enhanced the learning. I was learning with students so I could witness firsthand what did and did not work and what might be done to improve. Using role helped me engage in the fictional world with others and see how we "storied" (Clandinin and Connelly 2000) the worlds we co-constructed.

To learn most effectively, I agree with Heathcote (1994), teaching is best when it is negotiated. To negotiate successfully, a teacher must become a skillful facilitator within the classroom. There are times when process drama could be used as a told story, such as the *Titanic* experience, when I told my great uncle's story of being on the great ship through my grandmother's point of view. Still other times in the same process drama, the students needed to use stories to talk with Captain John Smith and not listen to a performed story. I needed to negotiate each choice to serve teaching. Is this a place for everyday or performed narratives? How can I use stories to increase learning?

As a teacher, I can change the way that narratives are used for teaching. A teacher can facilitate how narratives are used depending on context. Organized storytelling and stories used in a process drama context works differently. I see organized storytelling in the same way Agar (2005) views what he calls a "command and control organization" (27).

One teller runs the show. A narrative is tellable because the teller says so. It is not embedded in what the listener is doing—listeners stop what they're doing and gather around and listen. The story will be nice and linear, the clear and certain causal analysis you'd expect from the top of the hierarchy. The moral tone will be clear; no ambiguity or discussion allowed. (27).

In sharp contrast is the way that narratives operate when partnered with process drama or dramatic inquiry. Instead of storytelling and storymaking to serve performance goals, the real goal is sense making and making meaning using drama. Students did not enter the world of Bessie Coleman to tell her story, but instead to make sense as to why she could not fly in America. We watch and join in as many students in and out of role collectively make the story; "We'd hear contradictions and interruptions. Several people would be tellers" (Agar 2005, 27). We hear from the students who sympathize with Bessie's plight; we hear from those students in role who do not; we hear the story from the white, racist flight instructor as the teacher uses role to tell his story. Each story is embedded in what comes before and after its telling. From reading the children's book about Bessie, we are introduced to her brother's story both as a kid and as a grown-up. We placed this story in the larger drama to answer our curiosity as to why she could not fly in America.

Some stories might occur in the middle of the drama and reoccur; students might say, "Hey, did you see that? I told you that would happen, and it did." In the drama, story-based world, students can explore the possible, the probable, and even the improbable. The stories can occur in various places in planning, in the whole group, and from writing and/or drawing. The stories do not appear in a linear fashion, but from the point of curiosity. When one eases out, another one surfaces. The story does not end with one final telling, but instead continues as we explore the many reasons that Bessie Coleman was refused. The same occurs within the moral tone. Using process drama and dramatic inquiry, we do not tell the students, "Treating others differently because of their skin is wrong." Instead, they step into the world where it happens. As teachers, we guide them to make informed decisions, developing their moral understandings. In the end, "rather than a clear moral tone, it might be a dilemma" (27). They are left to wrestle with this dilemma and attempt to resolve what they think does not fit. This does not always work. They often can engage in this wrestling with other students, as they play using drama in the fictional world and as they question in the classroom world as well. Once again, I help negotiate their understanding and help them wrestle with their ideas so that they can freely discuss them. Teachers can learn to skillfully facilitate these dimensions of narrative to better inform their teaching both in the dramatic context and in the everyday world. Although I am examining these as separate categories, it is important to remember that these dimensions work in concert with each other.

It is essential when examining narrative to note the key differences between organized storytelling (Stone 1999) and storymaking (King 1993), although both are used frequently in process drama. In process drama, the stories, co-created to support the drama and not entertain an external audience, are always significant for student learning. As noted, in the mountain rescue process drama, the students constantly created stories together to rescue the injured mountain climber. However, they also relied on other ways to construct meaning including telling, writing, and drawing, which in turn introduced even more narratives. Students might talk while they draw and tell stories to communicate where they are and what they are wondering in both the drama and real worlds. Some of these narratives would be extended, developed, and even dropped, depending on the students' interest and direction within the drama. Stories extend the meaning in process drama, helping students visit the future possibilities. In organized storytelling, the teller's use of story is much more limited—telling in a performance to a listening audience. Process drama, however, invites exploration. Stories simply facilitate new learning that arises from the co-construction. In order to understand how a teacher might effectively use stories in process drama, one must look at how stories can be shaped and altered by changing the narrative dimension.

As a teacher, I need to use all the tools available, including narratives, to help students construct meaning. As a teacher, I am not limited to told stories, and my instruction should incorporate other ways to represent meaning. I also have to realize that narratives occur in many forms.

Process drama and dramatic inquiry have allowed me to expand my understandings and "test" my new identity. I did not have to subscribe exclusively to the rules of storyteller or teacher but was expected to suspend standard instruction to engage students with role and story co-construction within a drama world context to promote learning. I moved away from my more traditional and comfortable identities (storyteller, teacher) to use role, both fictional and real, to extend and strengthen my teaching capacity. Within this context, there are more learning possibilities. Students are not simply listening to a told story; they can interrupt the unfolding episodes to question, contest, or even change them. The teacher can facilitate the learning by entering the story and addressing the students in role. Students become invested when the work is both contextual and personal. In a sense, they are the storymakers of the fictional world, and they tell the story as it unfolds, sharing when they have something to question, address, or point out as significant. They are involved in the process of learning; whereas, in storytelling, the trancelike state (Strum 2000) is a desired outcome, but it is hard to predict if it is achieved for everyone. With process drama, the stories are created as they are made in the present, fictional time. As a teacher, one can see how much a student understands by how involved he or she is in the drama story-based world.

In examining my storytelling identity, I need to recognize others shaped it. Oring (1994) notes collective identity forms as a result of experience "that produces the deep sense of identification with others" (212). My introduction to process drama and dramatic inquiry changed my identity. First, as a storyteller, I wanted the students I worked with to see me as a storyteller. With process drama, I can be in role as someone who helps view and enact the dramatic world. My identity shifts as my role shifts. Using teacher-in-role and experiencing student-in-role changed my perspectives, creating a richer understanding of narrative as powerful agent for both storytelling and storymaking. Knowing how roles are used in process drama and dramatic inquiry, I realize I must shift my identity as I work with many groups for many reasons. Some hire me as storyteller, and still in my classes as a teacher of preservice teachers, I can negotiate my identities to match the teaching needs of my students.

Stories can simply be snapshot vignettes inviting discussion or even stopped and redirected by students or teacher as the teacher facilities new learning that arises from this co-construction. Narratives can be messy work, but it is in this disorder and discovery where meaning can be made. Teachers can shape and alter the dimensions of narrative to direct the learning. They need to ask: Would it help to add more tellers to this assignment? How much does this work complement other work? Am I teaching from a moralistic stance, or am I allowing students to develop moral understanding from their narrative interactions with other classmates?

This chapter details my trials and promises using stories and drama as an educator. I do this to improve my teaching. I now have more tools available for negotiation including both improvisation, and inquiry.

I have shifted my inquiry away from how a professional storyteller would attempt this or how I can create a tellable story from what we are working on. As I design my curriculum, I search from a broader perspective and deeper understanding of my new middle to incorporate ways to help students make meaning and, if possible, how to create meaning together.

Reflective writing has extended my understanding of identities, my role, and myself. It has allowed me to merge my identities to create a more mindful and informed pedagogy as I plan future curricula. The merging forms the new middle, a new understanding that does not neglect any past identity or present one that is still forming. While my teaching would certainly have evolved, this concentrated introspection allows me to synthesize my own learning not only creating deliberate applications for my instruction, but also allowing me to offer wider implications and future study recommendations for those beginning such a journey. As Richardson (1997) says, "Narrative displays the goals and intentions of human actors; it makes individuals, cultures, societies, and historical epochs comprehensible as wholes; it humanizes time; and it allows us to contemplate the effects of our actions and to alter the direction of our lives" (27).

In the following pages, I explain how my own professional storytelling has changed. As a professional storyteller presenting around the country and different parts of the world, I am using stories, blending elements of dramatic inquiry and process drama. Because of this, I believe I am a better teller. I have also used elements of storytelling, process drama, and dramatic inquiry to form what I would consider a "new middle" for these practices. I have changed to align my understanding of storytelling and storymaking and my new understanding of inquiry and improvisation for classroom instruction.

I have divided this method into two teaching approaches—ensemble storytelling for performance and ensemble storytelling for learning. In describing these experiences and changes, I will concentrate on how they have challenged my assumptions, introduced new tools and strategies I can call upon when working in each environment, and created significance for my students and myself with each approach. In order to explain, I use the following examples. For my own performance, I detail my own insight based upon various storytelling work experiences in both this country and Singapore.

1. To demonstrate ensemble storytelling for performance, I discuss the storymaking and storytelling involved in the storytelling experience with "The Flying Turtle" and "The Ghost of One Black Eye" and how working as an ensemble in the storymaking process heightens sociocultural learning.

2. To demonstrate ensemble story for learning, I highlight and chronicle my work alongside teacher Jonathan Fairman at the Cleveland School of the Arts teaching a unit on the *Titanic*.

Before I discuss these experiences, I address both the assumptions and tools developing with storytelling, dramatic inquiry, process drama, and storymaking. I have not disregarded my assumptions about told narratives completely, but within the last ten years, since I have been introduced to the profound ways process drama changes narrative, I continue to incorporate storytelling, storymaking, and dramatic inquiry into my work as a professional storyteller, dramatic inquiry teacher, and educator. Although some assumptions I have learned to revisit, there are others I struggle to release. Sometimes, I privilege told stories in the classroom. Although it took time, basic assumptions like all stories must have a beginning, middle, and end, I have abandoned to emphasize the value of the storymaking process for learning. Although I value Sawyer's tenets, I don't automatically use them. Instead, I question if the method will help me find new ways to use both silence and noise while respecting the time needed for storymaking.

Within the last eight years, I have begun blending storytelling, storymaking, process drama, and dramatic inquiry, so my work, both telling professionally and teaching, changes. In order to show this transformation, I draw upon specific experiences as a performer and educator.

As a professional storyteller, and now as someone who has specifically designed instruction using stories for learning with drama, what have I learned about using stories for learning that can connect to story for performance?

First, the essentials of storytelling, the tale, teller, and listener, change their relationships with one another when drama is introduced. As a performer, I do not always strive for the trancelike connection; instead, I find places to invite listeners and students to participate. This is not to say that I don't value the storytelling trance. I think it is an invaluable time to connect the teller and listener in a way that the moment of the story is in sync. However, I also believe connections can be made when the storymaking is highlighted and questions are asked. Professional storyteller Jay O'Callahan believes storytelling can be a lonely business, but, I question, does it have to be with this new perspective? In the role of a professional storyteller, I am the only one on stage telling to a listening audience. I hold the tellership. Whereas there are many listeners, there is only one teller who tries to create a trancelike state for listeners as they slip into the world of the story. Storytellers believe this experience is sacred and cannot be found in any other art form. I have witnessed trance and have been under one myself; however, when forming this new middle (Mora 1993) of understanding about how storytelling can operate, I learned to find places where the trance is not the desired result, but instead to transform the experience by involving more listeners in the telling process.

From working with the stories contained in process drama and dramatic inquiry, I have seen how students can engage in storymaking instead of merely listening to stories. For these reasons, I have shifted my own personal telling as a performer to include the audience as active agents in the experience. This way, they have a higher degree of tellership. I invite a more "active set of tellers" (Ochs and Capps 2001, 25). I weave improvisation into my telling performances. As noted, improvisational teaching is not easy, although it might appear effortless, and comes as a result of practice. Edmiston recommends a slow introduction to improvisation involving students in a five-minute process drama experience to gauge students' reactions. He believes teachers must evaluate these experiences with improvisation and build upon them with student input.

In this vein, I am finding ways to include improvisation in my storytelling work. As Heathcote (1984) states, improvisation is "discovering by trial, error and testing; using available materials with respect for their nature and being guided by this appreciation of their potential" (44). Although I cannot always use experience as the end product from improvisation, I can use it to improve the performance experience for both the students and me. For other storytellers, this might be to simply repeat some lines of a story or hold a few props and make sounds, but for me, it is to build story together. In other words, even though I am telling a told story for a listening audience, students are invited to engage in shaping some parts of the story with me. In the storytelling world, this is not common; it can become a new window of discovery to invite an active trance with the audience. Let me explain with an example.

I recently told for two thousand upper elementary students in a large theater for ninety minutes at Lorain Community College outside of Warren, Ohio. Because of the numbers and time limitations, I could not afford the personal attention for each student mirrored in process drama and dramatic inquiry. Instead, with my new understandings, I chose to work from the collective, meaning involving all students in the learning. In dramatic inquiry, all students can choose the same role. One of the first places I invite improvisation, where all students experience with me, is at the beginning where I set the conditions of the story. Before employing dramatic inquiry, I rarely spent enough time setting the tone for learning. In process drama and dramatic inquiry, students must be invited in and accept the invitation to join the fictional world. In the blending of the methods, as a performance teller, I can do this on a smaller scale in a larger theater. I use silence and breathing, literally asking students to breathe in and out for just a few seconds to transplant themselves into the setting of the story. I have them picture the story as I tell it. Using this contemplative time, I work so they enter the story with me before I start the story, deliberately increasing the tellability. Meaning becomes personal when they are invited to invest in the storymaking process as active agents. After each story, I have them collectively breathe again to help close one story and invite them to the next. For example, I might say, "Now that we have traveled to the place where Jack lives, please join with me as we travel to the back woods of West Virginia and discover the old man who does not want company." This is more than a simple, possibly unnecessary, introduction. It is an involved transition working with creating dramatic structures (O'Neill 1982) and dramatic inquiry (Edmiston 2007). I privilege the time it takes to transition from one moment to another, purposefully using drama conventions to help place each learning experience within the context in which it is studied. Storytelling need not be a solo art when process drama tools can be introduced to increase and sustain student engagement and learning.

Now, as I design stories, I search for places to invite improvisation with the audience. For example, in this same program, I told an African American and/or Appalachian tale called "Taileybone," also known as "TaileyPo" and "Most Peculiar Thing." Although not typically told with audience participation, I actually stop storylines to include ideas from the listening audience. I ask students to suggest names for the three dog characters, incorporating them into the story to increase involvement. I often improvise including many other story-based suggestions, agreeing with O'Neill (1982), who says that improvisation is at the heart of process drama. In order to improvise, I surrender the retelling of the fine details and concentrate on how I can make the experience significant for my listeners by personalizing the experience. I use students' names or invite students to share the stage—this is when storytelling comes alive. Professional storytellers pride themselves in creating a more direct connection with the audience. However, I suggest improvisation makes the audience a part of the stage, where the roles of teller and listener fuse. The improvisation not only includes audience members as performers, but also as shapers of story. Before, my storytelling programs, although not rigid, were prepared, and each story's direction was defined and known to me. For example, with an urban legend called "Gasoline Cat" and most recently an Anansi tale, "Where Stories Come From," I stopped the story at specific times, so students "paired and shared" ideas of what would happen. Similar to my work in process drama, I used their ideas not only as "talking points," but also as significant times to use improvisation as well. Improvisation is most effective when students tackle unsolved problems. Most recently, I have invited up to fifteen students to join me on stage to share their ideas, as we built a story around their responses. Before, I would see this as a break in the trance-like state storytellers create, but I realized this direct involvement with the tellers allows for a unique learning and performance experience. Although I incorporated student suggestions, I ended the performance with my pre-planned conclusion. I valued all suggestions, including them in the improvisational nature of our storytelling. Sometimes students provided ideas freely, while other times I invited the audience to echo back what was said. Clearly, I needed to mediate these choices to work them into the story.

As Vygotsky (1978) notes, when students engage in play, they learn more. When telling for a public performance, when I bring students on stage, I am careful to structure their ideas, so if it is seen as small, I make it more significant in the retelling. As I mediate these choices, I build student confidence, not only expanding their ideas, but also building them into the story. I might physically echo their story suggestions or incorporate them into moving tableaus borrowed from drama and dramatic inquiry or add mime and still pictures to illustrate their ideas. For example, I might use words that they say and give them power while I echo or have a group of students or the entire audience repeat them. They might say a creature was "as scary as the night," and we echo this collectively throughout the shared telling of the story. I also might create frozen pictures where the students demonstrate a time when they are scared and use that same froze picture when telling the story. When I bring students on stage to help other students, I try to use scaffolding (Bruner 1978) to increase their comfort levels.

Edmiston suggests teaching for students on the edge of learning. These are the students who are not actively involved in the classroom—the ones "sitting on the edge" of learning. As Edmiston had told me, if we can reach these children, we can reach everyone. We are taught to reach all abilities, but we often do not because students are forgotten. In that vein, I bring any student who wants to be involved in the telling on stage with me. This makes it possible to co-construct and co-author the story with an audience. Improvisation is powerful. It takes careful mediation to create a comfort level with students to tell with me, not for me, creating together. On one such occasion, I ended my program by inviting the entire faculty to improvise a story together based upon students' suggestions. I allowed the story to change with each teller. I was less a storyteller and more of a mediator for the story and the tellers. Teachers often improvised new ways of representing the story themselves—dancing, singing, or even adding mime. Improvisation has changed me as a professional storyteller; I look for opportunities to create spaces for students to express their ideas and understandings.

In my other organizing roles in storytelling, I have concentrated on told stories. For more than twenty-five years, the National Storytelling Network (NSN) has considered me an advocate for youth storytelling. I have trained and assisted youth and youth leaders with storytelling performance. I founded YES, Youth, Educators, and Storytellers Special Interest Group, for NSN with the hopes to unite educators and youth to explore other possible methods of using story. I, along with a few others, helped create a "Youthful Voices" tent, with standing room only capacity for more than seventeen hundred people, telling under the tent at the National Storytelling Festival, and for three years served as the executive director for the National Youth Storytelling Olympics, a nationwide event to showcase youth storytellers. These events were milestones for youth storytelling. However, they still were to help tellers as solo tellers, not incorporating collaborative telling. I had always wished there were more ways to show the value of youth storytelling and storymaking. I began to include more youth in my performance work, combining ideas of process drama and dramatic inquiry into performance telling. I was attracted to the way whole groups could be engaged in storytelling. I created a method that used groups of people in the storytelling process plus incorporate improvisation and mediation. I call this ensemble storytelling for performance.

When I refer to an ensemble, I mean a group of students who use story to explore and question the story world they create together.

Neelands (2009) discusses ensemble in relation to process drama where students "adopt a pro-social ensemble-based process for building community and a common culture" (175). When students engage in a fictional world, they use real world understandings to relate to it. They are able to test what it means to build community, and in role, they become someone else, deciding with others how to move into the world. When students are working in an ensemble, as they create a story, they also learn how to live in the story and manage in the real world working with students. As Neelands stresses, they learn "the grave importance of our interdependence as humans" (176). My goals in creating ensemble storytelling are not to simply co-construct a story, but to experience with the students that learning how to live in a fictional world can apply to the real world. By working with fictional roles, they are also able to see what does not work as well. Each co-constructed narrative is weighed against ideas and negotiated. These are values any teacher would like to address with students. When done in a concerted or ensemble method, they are not reminded what it means to be democratic in their living—they experience it.

As I began developing these methods, I involved all students, not just those with a penchant for performing or stories. This is why I ask teachers, when working with this method, to provide twenty to thirty students—any level and any ability—to tell. Before, I would use a few stories, have them practice, and then showcase a few of the students telling for the class. Using the ensemble storytelling for a performance method, I now can involve all of the students in both the storymaking and storytelling processes. I struggled with the idea of highlighting performance as an outcome. Using this method, the product is a performance that highlights process as well. The process also serves to create the product, the final tellable story.

On one hand, this contradicts the tenets of process drama and dramatic inquiry, because it involves a viewed performance by people who are not part of the telling. This method, too, serves to expand some of the tenets such as improvisation and mediation in drama to include performance. I had to weigh my options. Many teachers want a performance. They, like in my past, understood this was the result for storytelling. I had to rethink and create a method to involve performance but also use what I had learned about process-based learning to create an educational experience. I wished to find a way to allow many students to take part in creating or making the story for performance. When stories are uttered, even story fragments, they are considered performed (Bauman 1978). What is important is how the stories are used with the students. This is why I created two methods, one that includes performance, called ensemble storytelling for performance, and one for learning, called ensemble story learning. I wanted to be able to inform teachers stories are not just for performance, they can be used to design and create curricula as well.

ENSEMBLE STORYTELLING FOR PERFORMANCE

In my previous organized storytelling workshops, we examined stories with a clear-cut beginning, middle, and end. However, with ensemble storytelling for performance, I co-create stories with the students. I work with twenty or more students for a little under an hour (it is difficult for teachers to give me more time than this) to co-create a story for performance. Sometimes teachers are only able to work between bell schedules. Starting with a storytelling skeleton, we build a story to share with other students. Student inquiry can take any direction, but like dramatic inquiry, all ideas are heard and incorporated if possible. Working with students in this fashion is certainly a risk but calculated. When working with a story called "The Flying Turtle," a student suggested we tie the turtle to an airplane. Even though this did not fit with the folktale, we did it. I was surprised when I found things we could use in the story from this reenactment. In order to start this drama, I first shared a told story.

I minimize the expression, simply sharing the tale and emphasizing we have an hour to build "beyond the bones."

In other words, we add our voices and choices to the making and telling of these stories. This means there were more tellers offering how we should co-construct the narratives. As Heathcote says of improvisation, we use trial and error methods to create our story together. Facilitating and improvisation are tools that allow discovery to create a tellable, shared story developed in the tight span of ninety minutes. It is difficult to build from every idea, but I work to include them all. Also, like in process drama and dramatic inquiry, in my mind, I operate from the physical and fictional world. In the physical world, the classroom, I am ever conscious of the time we have to prepare, rehearse, and perform. In the fictional world, we explore ideas as characters in the story. Although this work does have a continual, narrative strand, we are constantly mediating even in the final minutes. Let me illustrate.

In one school visit, we created a version of "The Flying Turtle," an old folktale found in many cultures detailing how the turtle first cracks his shell and subsequently why all turtles have had cracks since. After telling a bare bones version, I introduce new information—the turtle wants to fly. As the students introduce four or five story fragments as to how the turtle might fly—with the help of birds and other such examples—we enact them. Instead of one or two students explaining the idea, we have one person explain and then we all use drama to present. We immediately step into role as the characters and make it real. Each student presents a choice, and I mediate each one. I found the best way to represent and provide a frame is to enter the drama. Students also introduce storylines—maybe he should tie a rocket on his back, superglue feathers to his shell, strap himself to an airplane, or even tie himself to a bomb. All ideas are explored, considered, and, using drama, enacted. In the last suggestion, I did not disregard the bomb choice, but, instead, we collaboratively co-authored how we might attach the bomb and what might happen as a result. Even though, I have to admit, sometimes I do not think it will work, the students have always shown me through their improvisational structuring how to rethink and reinvent story. In their roles as characters in the story, we discuss how it can work. In the end, the turtle eventually bit on a stick held by the birds but opened his mouth and fell to the Earth. He cracked his shell as a result. However, as I mediated the students' ideas, we found ways to work as an ensemble in the delivery of the story's ending. In one telling, we had as many as ten turtles, the rest birds, using drama to represent what happened, and in another we had one turtle, the rest birds.

I try to avoid one student playing a central role; instead, we switch roles around, so students have a variety of experiences within the story. With my mediation, I make sure every student is involved both in the making and the telling of story. Sometimes there are many turtles or a guest appearance from a bear—regardless, all of these ideas change and move with the co-constructions of story. As students understand all ideas are accepted, they become even more creative with presentation and performance. As someone mediating the ideas, one must be careful in organizing how it is structured. Learning to use improvisation, the "teacher-imposed structure and intervention is not antithetical to successful improvisation; in fact, they are critical ingredients. The trick is in knowing what kind, how much and when to impose structure" (Wagner 1990, 195). In order to determine this, I listen well, and I respond to all ideas that the students have as we start to co-construct a story. Using this method, I need to decide when to enter the world with the students, when to step into classroom world to make a point, and how to use intervention and structure to build engagement. I remember a student offered up that we could use a rocket launcher, and this worked. We were able to boost the turtle by having other students strap the rocket launcher on his back. However, my role of story mediator was challenged when a student said that he should be equipped with a guitar because he can "fly when he is hearing music." As the mediator of the story, I had to make the choice whether using the metaphor of flying would enhance or deter the story. However, drawing from Heathcote (1990), we negotiated, and the students were able to have the turtle play the guitar while the birds carried him. He flew, the student's suggestion being honored, but at the same time, he also physically flew in the story.

I needed to provide spaces for improvisation for the development of stories and those involved in making and telling the story.

After this story, we told and used drama to enact another story. However, it had not been prepared. I knew the bones of the story, but, using improvisation, the students helped create the direction and action. It was truly improvised by us and mediated by me. I asked if they wanted to tell another story, but with no practice, we improvised an ensemble performance of "The Ghost of One Black Eye." I simply provided the instruction: "Build from whatever I suggest or say." I reminded students, all shared ideas are valued. We often invited other students, or even faculty members, into the performance. I mediated the delivery, although a simple ghost story with a direction and plotline known to me, it changed with the introduction of the improvisational choices of the students and invited guests. Students physically acted out the work, but along the way, we heard dialogue not from the original tale. I challenged myself to let go of being the solo teller, becoming one who made sure story was experienced by students and audience as they both created and performed. I have to admit when I first started, the story would slip into simply retelling what I provided, but as I let go of the story and the intended direction, I learned students could really build from the frame. As we practiced the story, the students made suggestions such as, "I will lock the door, and the ghost cannot enter." As story mediator, instead of saying no to this idea, I simply created a way for the ghost to walk through the door but used the student's suggestion and kept the door locked. I did not plan on the ghost walking through the door, and it did add more surprise to the story as it was shared.

In improvisational storytelling, the teller becomes a story "mediator" (Vygotsky 1978) using the story ideas, story fragments, and multiple story improvisations suggested by students as he or she co-directs the development of the story. The story mediator does not have to tell stories but, instead, can fill the silence or steer the direction of the story drama. Students must feel safe physically and comfortable enough to be involved. I allow stories to blossom and intervene when they stray from the story's problem or when a student stumbles in delivery.

One student wished to tie a firecracker to the turtle, a bottle rocket, so he could fly higher. The students did not hear the idea, so I stopped the drama and, in the real world, invited the student to repeat it, and in my role as facilitator, I positioned the student to have authority to address questions from his aide. An idea that originally could not be heard, due to this teaching move, proved to be significant as we developed this story. As an ensemble (I performed as well) we learn and perform together. Using this method, I can see students learning from each other by the choices they make as they build the performance together.

However, since the work is designed for performance, we work to create the performance. The students learn from reactions from the audience, and I provide "Cordi notes" on what went well to improve and direct learning and future inquiry.

At the National Youth Storytelling Olympics, the National Storytelling Festival, and my work with students in storytelling as a storytelling coach for more than twelve years, I was not able to have students really engage in the storymaking process as much as when I use ensemble storytelling for performance. We created what we performed together. Before, students would learn a story and perform it alone for an audience. Using this method, I am able to incorporate a sociocultural approach (Vygotsky 1978) to storymaking. The students work together and decide how to create a tellable story from their own ideas and suggestions, and I can help "scaffold" (quoting Bruner 1978) the experience. This was not possible when youth told stories as a solo activity. This experience increases the learning potential by including more tellers, adding more improvisation, and using mediation for learning with the storymaking and storytelling process.

Ensemble storytelling for performance is one way to use stories and drama. It is designed to build a performance together. However, I want teachers to realize using stories with drama can be possible for teaching and learning, however, as a storyteller, I realize I do lean toward using narratives in order to highlight learning. The teacher part of my identity pulls me into the middle. This is why I have offered and have taught my approach using ideas from process drama and dramatic inquiry called ensemble story learning.

ENSEMBLE STORYTELLING FOR LEARNING

Picture a classroom where the student thinks and act as an engineer on the *Titanic*. One student is concerned about what type of material was used to build the hull, another wonders about the impact of the iceberg, and all the others are wondering just how to explain why it sank on that terrible night. In a few days, they will have to explain it to the press. There is a nervous tension surrounding the meeting, but everyone has an investment in being able to tell us the story. This is what happened when teacher Jonathan Fairman and I co-constructed a story-based drama at the Cleveland School for the Arts using ensemble story learning.

First, we understood this method was new for both of us. We were fashioning our understanding before, during, and after the experience, which was scheduled to take a few days. We decided we would use a told and tellable story to invite the students into the fictional world.

Like in process drama, the story would serve as a pre-text (O'Neill 1982) to invite student engagement in the world of drama. Fairman and I were interested in using storytelling and storymaking with this group of students building upon the dramatic approach of process drama because it employs students as experts in shaping the stories they share. Drawing from Heathcote, students do not take on this work as students, but as people who would be invested in the field, engineers. The perspective should be from the engineer's view. In this case, they were all engineers who helped build the *Titanic*. Like in dramatic inquiry, student curiosity drove the drama. Although told stories were privileged in this drama, other methods were used to enact the stories. We preferred told stories as a way for students to construct meaning because both Fairman and I were storytellers who wanted to see how providing space for told stories and creating told stories could help accelerate the learning using drama.

However, unlike storytelling, we were interested in the everyday stories in the fictional world as well. It is the unraveling (Ochs and Capps 2001) from possible story fragments that sustain student interest. As a teacher-in-role, as one of the engineers, and, at times, as the person preparing the meeting for the press, I used stories not only to enter the fictional world, but also to sustain the drama with the students.

In my previous work with process drama and dramatic inquiry, we generally did not work with a told story performed by a story-teller to enact the drama. In this case, I would tell a true story to start the investment and invitation to learn more about the *Titanic*. To inspire interest, I told my grandmother's *Titanic* story. She once told me, "Your great uncle died on that big boat. I think it was famous." I told this story as though I were a young boy in West Virginia. In the story, I shared how I spent the next few years trying to authenticate this story—searching to discover if my great uncle really died on the *Titanic*. In the story, I explained how years later, when I went to the Center for Science and Industry's *Titanic* exhibit, I found that my great uncle indeed had died, but my great aunt, who I did not know existed, had lived. This tellable story and my personal journey were the entrance points for the students to ask further questions about other stories concerning the *Titanic*. From here we laid out books, articles, and maps, and students wrote on Post-it notes what they found out and what they knew. I developed a story exercise called I Wonder and I Was Curious. We asked the class to tell a story based on what they had discovered, placing it in a frame of a story using "I wonder." Students said, "I wonder, how many people died? "I was curious was there really a 'heart of the ocean' (from the popular movie)?" "I wonder, why did it sink?" or "I wonder, was anyone at fault?" Students shared at least two facts about the story using this frame. After this, we invited them into a fictional world of the *Titanic* and asked them to consider what roles they wished to play.

Some examples of students' stories included: "It was cold, very cold, on the *Titanic*. It says people died because of the severe cold in the water. I wonder, did they recover many bodies?"

Others said, "I heard the youngest survivor was only four months old. Does he remember anything about that terrible night? I wonder, what would he tell us right now about it?"

We framed these questions inside narratives. These story frames became the inquiry points helping us determine areas of curiosity and learning. We decided who we would like to be, and what we would like to discover. Because students were most concerned as to why the ship sank, we became engineers. One student responded:

My specialty was construction of the boat. Sir, when we were going out to buy the wood, I received a telegram from Mr. Smith, and he said we don't have enough money for the wood. I went out and bought the wood and noticed that this wood was flimsier than the wood we were supposed to buy. The iceberg actually cut the wood and might have been because we could not get the other wood

This student's story led to other stories and questions. Students informed other students that the ship had been built from steel, not wood. They questioned how the rivets were made and wondered if cheap rivets could have caused the ship to sink. Some students, in role, began to defend the rivets, while others questioned if buying cheaper wood might have caused the ship to sink. Being the story mediator, I was also able to have them search and read from the recently released work that blamed the rivets as a major contribution to why it sank. In preparing this ensemble story-based inquiry, I made sure to continue my research on the *Titanic*, including recent events and work.

In my role, I used mediation and improvisation to prepare a fictional environment. In other words, the fictional place was where stories were heard. An example of this would be a courtroom; we expect to hear told stories there. In this case, the place was an organized meeting. In their roles as engineers, they prepared for a meeting to address the press. I used parliamentary procedure to recognize students who wanted to share their stories as experts. This format allowed for tellable narratives to surface. An example of this follows.

> TEACHER (in role): "All right, this meeting starts at 2:15 p.m.; can you check your clocks please? We are going to be here for a long time. Did we bring drinks? Who was responsible for the drinks?"
>
> STUDENT: I was.
>
> TEACHER (in role): We are going be here for a while because we have something to figure out. We built this ship. We are getting a lot of flak from the press. We have many people who want to know why it sank. I am not blaming anyone here, because I helped build this ship. We have engineers; we have steel workers; you have done the research. Can you tell us possible reasons for why this ship went down?

Parliamentary procedure outlined a speaking order. Because of this, each student who wanted to speak could. The stories told at the meeting surfaced from their curiosity. The student who wanted to talk about the rivets became an expert on rivets. We had an iceberg specialist tell us how the iceberg looked that night, detailing how cold it was.

In another example, I used story to transform the environment when students wanted to speak to Captain Edwin John Smith to help comfort him. Initially, they yelled responses to him, but a student whispered, "God will provide." Some students laughed, so I changed the environment so Captain John Smith (student-in-role) and the students' suggestions would be more accepted. I said, "Wait, listen, look around. There is mist around the captain. If you look closely, I believe I see a tear in Captain Edwin John Smith's eye. Look at him. I believe he is sad. Imagine if you were him right now. Your ship and many of the passengers have just met their fate at the bottom of the ocean. The same people you just smiled at and maybe shared a drink, and now look at him." I then stepped into the world of the classroom and using told stories said, "When I read about Smith, most said he went down with the ship. Others said they saw a ghost of him for many years, and when they saw him as a ghost, he reached out and tried to say something." I was pleasantly surprised when students mirrored this. Then I went back to the fictional world, showing that told stories are useful for everyday and fictional worlds. I said, "As you walk by, in a whisper say something comforting if you like. If you don't want to say words, show by your face that you are with him. You don't have to walk, but those that do, come now." Some students then moved toward the captain and whispered words of support, while others stayed where they were. After that, the tone of the class was more caring and reverent. I had changed the environment so the stories shared would be more respected and mediated the conversation so the student-in-role as the captain would not hear screams but feel support. I told a story in the fictional world that changed how students saw the captain.

Using stories changed not only the environment, but also how the students engaged within the drama. We started with a told story of my grandmother, from there shaped an environment to invite stories, and used altered environments to shift the stories. This showed me told stories have more value than those performed. We also used narrative fragments to help promote further questions and heighten the investment by exploring and investigating our work. We were not simply asking questions about the fictional world; we were acting on those questions—we wanted to find out and so we explored. Along the way, we shared stories.

I wondered what other ways I could employ the tenets of dramatic inquiry and process drama in storytelling.

ADJUSTMENTS

It is not always a clear-cut decision which method to use with students. Sometimes, I am confused whether to use ensemble story for performance, ensemble story learning, process drama, or inquiry. I still blend these ideas. In fact, the most significant time in my teaching with process drama happened when I did not plan to use it.

A rural Catholic school invited me as a storyteller and workshop presenter. The librarian knew my advisor and knew I taught classes in process drama. She made an assumption that what I learned in process drama I could do as a storyteller. She did not separate the two. In casual conversation, I informed her about my work using process drama concerning the subject of the *Titanic*. Little did I know what I did for 25 students would transfer to more than 220 students. I did not plan to use process drama with more than 200 students. I planned to provide a told story workshop. I had to think on my feet and change the way that I intended to teach. I let go of the main constructs of storytelling, and instead of preparing for a performance, I prepared for mass learning. I divided the groups from various grade levels into smaller groups, still quite large, consisting of 10 to 15 per group. Using a microphone was quite useful to keep their interests moving. I prepared 10 to 15 small process-drama experiences in a large gym. This was not easy. I tried, sometimes in vain, to keep the students thinking about what they were curious about concerning the *Titanic*, one of the central goals of dramatic inquiry. I tried to use their curiosity to find out more. It was difficult to have more than 200 students use tableau at the same time. We did this at first—students were quiet, listening to what each scene depicted. However, soon, they wanted to explore more on their own. I found what would bring them back to learning more about the *Titanic* was to work not toward the inquiry but toward performance. I had one person per group narrate the choices. At the end, we told our stories in a storytelling format where students would share their tableaus but tell the stories of before and after the tableau. This experience taught me to be willing to let go and adapt to the needs of the learners. I also learned that the arrangements can play a significant role in making this decision.

In all of this work, whether it happens when I perform alone or with other students, it is the reflection upon these experiences that has built my direction for change in my future. As a teacher, I am involved in reflection in both the fictional and the real worlds. This reflection leads to further improvisation and helps me realize when I need contact points for mediation. Contact points are times that it is necessary to switch a role, provide a transition, or heighten tension in the drama or story.

I am currently serving on the National Advisory Board for Teaching Tolerance part of the Southern Law Poverty Center. Using what I have learned from this organization, I am in the process of combining storytelling, ensemble storytelling to address the topic of anti-bullying. After reading the book *Wonder* by R. J. Palacio (2012), we have created the "Wonder Team," and this year (2017–2018) we have visited schools to teach about these issues. We have created ensemble drama work. In this work, students in role use drama to be parents deciding during a school board meeting if Auggie, a boy with facial deformities who is central to the story, should stay in school. I have led this ensemble work with my college students many times, and I am now realizing the value in preparing these preservice educators using this pedagogy. I want them to experience more using drama to employ the "teacher-in-role" and mediate the story. This is one way that I can help teachers in training know about this work and use it in their future classrooms. In a recent presentation (2018) at the Ohio Council Teachers of Language Arts

Conference, my students and their parents used drama to enact the role of Auggie. However, they engaged in other roles, such as a principal, a secretary, or someone in the news because it served the drama. Watching me model this before and giving them permission, they began to see and use role and other dramatic conventions to promote inquiry. However, more than that, they began in role to ask more of the participants. Before they simply waited for me to give them an action, but as we progress, they are taking action on their own. For example, as Auggie's parents, they asked for people to be sensitive to the responses and condition of Auggie because he was scheduled for surgery after the meeting. This tension allowed a new form of talk, more caring talk, with Auggie and his parents.

As we travel, the students are waiting for me less and less to mediate; instead, they are engaging students with their narrative leads. I intend to continue this because I can see how this can lead to future practitioners of narrative-led teachers.

This work is about change, and how I have seen the identity of "storyteller" and "teacher who uses stories" grows, expands, and transforms to incorporate many new understandings informed by drama and dramatic inquiry. I understand more about who I am and how my new middle changes with each teaching and personal experience. Instead of struggling to define the change, I embrace and welcome it. I know understanding this change helps inform who I am, who I can be, and who I will be.

Harrison (2002) affirms how telling your story can be powerful to helping one know who he or she is:

> This storytelling work—and it is difficult—is remarkably, rewarding and healthy. As we reveal ourselves in story, we become aware of the continuing core of our lives under the fragmented surface of our experiences. As we become conscious of the multifaceted, multi-chaptered "I" who is the storyteller, we can trace out the paradoxical and even contradictory versions of ourselves that we create for different occasions, different audiences—and the threads that weave all these

chapters, all three versions into the whole. Most important, as we become aware of ourselves as storytellers, we realize that we understand
and imagine about ourselves in a story. (74)

In order to be a better teacher, I must engage in the private reflections to make public differences. Witherell and Noddings (1991)
suggest, "The power of narrative and dialogue as contributors to
reflective awareness in teachers and students is that they provide
opportunities for deepened relations with others" (8). They argue,
"Teaching is both a public and private activity. It calls on both narrative and analytic ways of knowing . . . The act of teaching calls us
to live in the worlds of actuality and of possibility and vision" (9).

At the forefront of using storytelling, storymaking, process
drama, and dramatic inquiry is student-centered learning. However, I need to reflect for each class how best to use these methods. Each method is not scripted, but instead a complex system
of learning that depends upon the relationship between students
as learners. As Shuman (1988) notes, "Storytelling offers one of its
greatest promises, the possibility of empathy, of understanding
others" (180). Whether a student is telling a fictional tale or a real
one, students are given an outlet to perform, share, and present
with other students. And in telling my stories, I, too, feel I know
my students more. I am able to share the learning and experience
it alongside them.

Storytellers have followed the basic tenets of storytelling set
forth by Ruth Sawyer. However, this study challenges the role of
the storyteller, the way story is seen, and how it is used for teaching.
It suggests as storytellers we need to value both storymaking and
storytelling when we are in the classroom. Both are forms of performance, and merely because a story is not performed does not mean
it does not have value. We need to become more improvisational
in our work, especially when the stories are used for teaching purposes. Storytelling teachers need to expand the way they use stories
and value the connection of process drama and story.

At a time when artists are appearing less and less in the classroom due to budget constraints, it becomes important to value and extend how story is used for teaching. Telling a story has immense value, but so does engaging in the world of story. Storytellers need to sometimes take risks and experiment with story.

As a result of this study, the following implications could be and should be considered in the storytelling community.

1. Expanding the position of storyteller in academia and education. Storytellers followed the tenets set by Ruth Sawyer, but these tenets applied to performance storytelling within organized storytelling. However, as more and more storytellers are invited into university and school settings, we need to show the connections between performance and meaning making with narrative. I hope this study invites curiosity and encourages more storytellers to re-examine their own methods and find intersections and connections with classroom curricula that are more than simply entertainment or one-time storytelling performances. Storytellers can partner with teachers to make mindful choices to co-construct learning and create sustained student inquiry. Through further scholarship and investment, storytellers can forge new, innovative relationships that bridge storytelling as an art to storytelling and storymaking as educational practices to increase teaching using narratives.

2. Challenging storytellers to step out of the box. From working in the field and with a national organization and international storytellers, I know storytellers are often guarded and protective of what storytelling means. They clearly follow an organized definition of storytelling. However, valuing the interactive nature of stories helps expand how storytellers are used in the field. This is true only if the teller is willing to allow it to be interactive. Storytellers are now being called to work in businesses, social justice centers, and nursing homes, where performance is not always the desired outcome. Instead, one needs to value stories, both in storytelling and storymaking as community-building tools to help give voice to those often silenced. Using storytelling and storymaking with process drama allows adults and students to be someone else to be heard in the fictional world. However, as was noted, this use of stories shows the transfer of what is learned in the fictional world can also be applied to the real-world context.

3. Use process drama in storytelling. The storytelling community needs to invite, encourage, learn, and challenge themselves to use drama, namely process drama and dramatic inquiry or ensemble storytelling, as they work with students. In a standard-based education, stories can be used to engage students in productive inquiry and sustained learning. The needs of the teachers are not the same as those of the storytellers, but hopefully as storytellers become more and more invested in the continual work in the classroom, more negotiation can result. If storytellers want to work more in the schools, they need to be willing to examine stories in different ways than they are used to seeing them. When used in a dramatic context, students and the storyteller can imagine and enact the story not from a position of authority but as co-constructors. This provides more possibilities for storytellers to be included in classroom curricula.

4. Storytellers need to value the storymaking and see the performative quality in this work. From working with professional storytellers for more than twenty years, they would not view storymaking as having a performance element to the process. However, as Bauman (1967) and Langellier and Peterson (2004) note, interactive narratives are performed. Storytellers can expand their work in the classroom if they value creating narratives or storymaking as much as storytelling in performance settings. We need to listen more and employ pedagogies of process drama and dramatic inquiry to see how the goal of using storytelling and storymaking can serve learning, not performance.

5. The value of improvisation. As Heathcote (1994) notes, improvisation is key to process drama. This is true of storytelling and especially storymaking. After working with process drama and dramatic inquiry, I can see how working with the audience as active agents in shaping the story increases story investment. Many storytellers rely on the audience's facial expressions to determine the direction of their telling. However, a more immediate feedback is to include them in the story, not simply using repetition or adding words in an echo format, but actually using improvisation to help shape the story. If more storytellers use improvisation in their work, they can expand their work with students, and their performances as well. It was when I risked performing my stories and opened up the possibilities for my audience to help me shape them that my storytelling took on new directions. I now try to find places in the story that we can improvise

together. If more storytellers use dramatic play in their work, they will see stories from the vantage point of possibilities to explore and develop and not always as a performed work.

6. The value of process drama and dramatic inquiry. As storytellers, our work is narrative. Process drama and dramatic inquiry and ensemble storytelling depend upon narratives. They cannot happen without them. We need to invest in this form of narrative, so we can expand what we offer in the classroom. With process drama, students can step into the world of the story and question it. With dramatic inquiry, students can question and can engage in their questions by using role to challenge their inquiry. Storytellers need to search for stories that meet these requirements. However, if more and more storytellers use process drama and dramatic inquiry and ensemble storytelling, they will be involved with students in creating, shaping, and directing how narratives are used to help students learn. Storytellers can expand and redefine what it means to be a storyteller. Instead of one who simply tells stories, one can step in and engage in the stories with the students. The trancelike state (Strum 2000) can become a true transformation as an active state where students shape and build the stories they imagine.

7. The importance of reflection. Folklorist/storyteller Ruth Stotter once said there is no unified schooling for storytellers—anyone can call himself or herself a storyteller. Over the years, I have seen storytelling in many forms. I have seen some tellers simply echo the same program year after year. However, the storytellers I admire most are the ones that critically examine their work. In a sense, critical writing or at least deep self-reflection and growth are reflected in their work. I can see how they have been changed, altered, and transformed by story selection. I note the critical discussions and analysis in their work as they prepare. This mindfulness sets them apart and in a real sense advances storytelling to a higher level. Unfortunately, storytellers are often too busy or do not understand the value in writing about their work. Only now are storytellers realizing with the deaths of such storytelling pioneers as Ray Hicks, Brother Blue, Jackie Torrence, and Syd Lieberman, our art needs to be chronicled, challenged, and expanded. Deep writing encourages tough questions, introspection, and the informed realization

of a new middle. Storytellers should challenge themselves to such an
introspection to understand their art and contribute to its scholarship.

As a teacher and storyteller, with each decision, I attempted to
sustain the engagement between my worlds. In both worlds, I realize I must work to master my craft. However, it is only by critically
reflecting that this can be achieved. I must take time to not strad-
dle the world of a professional teller and that of a classroom and
university teacher, but instead to dive deep into not only my past
work but also my present. I use the past to inform my present. This
critical work allows me to do so.

My family guides me. My students guide me. Jack guides me.
They serve not only as an audience, but also as participants in my
writing. I write of me but also of them. They inform my teaching.
Their stories are as strong as mine.

I have found that the access keys are not always visible. Like Jack,
I have to seek out to understand the worlds I am in. Writing allowed
me to revisit, resee, and reenergize my craft. The depth of my writing depends on my self-reflection. My voice in this relied on my
understanding by my social groups, the ones I willingly joined, the
ones I was admitted to, and the ones that I had to work to understand and eventually gain admittance.

However, in this work, I learned not to value one voice or identity
over another. Instead, I privileged the identity of storyteller when it
needs to be. The same applied to the identity of educator. I also realized there were times when I drew upon both to inform me. When
I need to speak with an academic flair, I am not neglecting that the
storyteller resides in me. Instead, I wrestle to find new places for
story to be admitted. Jack guides me.

I do not simply list the event, I do not hide my feelings. They guide
me. As much as they guided Jack to get him out of trouble, expressing
my feelings brings me closer to my work, my students, and myself.

I teach my students by listening and hearing stories. I realize
that when I use stories of vulnerability, such as the found journal

or Vanessa's getting jumped into a gang, I teach my students to see these stories not from an evaluative stance, but instead from a listening one. This story is not only about teaching me to deeply listen, but also to teach my students not to pass judgment on others. Instead, there is room for all stories.

As our nation tries to standardize learning or provide prescriptive formulas that try to civilize us or make us all represent some illusive "core," we need to value the richness that comes from listening, especially listening to stories of difference. Each story detailed here requires a special kind of listening. In order to hear Vanessa's story, one must listen to the truth that "no" is not an option in joining the gang in her street. As an educator, I use stories instead of strategies and the way that I use stories depends on who is listening to them. I am not looking for strategies that will work across all classroom teaching; instead I draw on my story, other stories, and most importantly, the story of the students I work with to decide how to use narratives to teach them. Perhaps we all need to listen a little more instead of trying to test everyone the same way. Jack is here to guide you and me.

My story is still being told. Like Jack, I am still seeking my fortune. Like Jack, it is the journey that is the reward. According to Lindhal (2001), in his book *Perspectives on the Jack Tales and Other American Marchen*, "It is less the job of the hero than of the plot. Story structure is in many ways simply an externalization of the inner rewards of virtue. The hero's riches come as a reward for simply being who he or she is—when no one else is watching" (77).

I am on my Jack journey. The rewards are in the pursuit. I have been richly rewarded by looking back at my work as a storyteller and story teacher. I am not seeking gold or magical tricks, but instead of being more aware of how use my collective identities as a teller and teacher. I also want to help others start their Jack journey. After all, the Jack story is our story. Even when Richard Chase, the most famous collector of Jack tales set out to personalize the Jack tales as his own, he found out that they belong to all of us. Or as Perdue (2001) states, "Through Richard Chase, Appalachian Jack became American Jack" (125). My American tale was never a solo one. Instead, I wish that my tale brings you closer to your Jack journey. I invite you if you are a classroom teacher, dive into the art of telling stories as a form of teaching and if you are teller, redefine how you use stories and find new methods to entertain and to teach using narratives. As much as Jack continues to seek out his fortune, I search for mine.

> Jack is a kind of trickster-hero, one who is successful through his cleverness. Certainly he is not the admirable prince of fairy tales, but rather a quick witted and not always too scrupulous farm boy. In these tales as told in Appalachia Jack is an ordinary poor boy who achieves success in only one of two ways: either by his wits, or by sheer luck— and the latter predominates. Quite a contradiction to the "American fairy tale" mythos that honesty and hard work are the means to success! (http://www.appalachianhistory.net/2016/04/jack-tales-not -just-beanstalks.html)

In writing, I do not need to not use my wits, but, instead, I need to be clever—clever, not in the sense of being tricky, but place a smart focus on my work and my understanding of my work. It is not a fairytale, but instead a folk narrative of struggle, finding help, and seeking out understanding.

Like Jack, I need to be clever, so I can see what I need to see and not neglect new ways that story can be used. As Sobol (1992) states in the introduction to *Southern Jack Tales*, "There are Jack tales, in which Jack takes on the mythic attributes of a shaman, or culture hero, by moving freely between natural and spiritual worlds, subduing evil, restoring harmony, and bringing back blessings to the community" (14). I can't think of a better blessing than finding new methods for students to learn and preparing educators, like myself, to teach.

In this next journey, I will continue to use writing as a critical lens to value my work as a storyteller, teacher, and process drama teacher. I know that in writing I understand how my identity continues to be in flux. As I reflect upon my journey as an educator, I relax, pause, and take respite because I know by staying still, I move forward. In this work, I held still the importance of the essential elements of storytelling and storymaking, that is, tale, teller, and listener. However, as they stayed still, I did not. I wrestled, in my mind and in my writing, with how I could change, and as I prepare to continue to use stories and drama for both performance and teaching, I am willing and eager to change again.

Orville Hicks (2009), a descendent of the well-known teller Ray Hicks, in his book *Jack Tales*, comments:

I guess, the new generation coming on.
Jack might be a thing of the past
I mean, as far as telling. (37)

I say, as much as Jack tricked his way into my classroom, so it is with storytelling. He is simply finding new ways to enter our classroom. Whether it is using drama or not, he is waiting for us to notice he is there. Storymaking and storytelling enable students to learn. Story has a firm place in the classroom, and only when we begin to use it for our students will we truly find our fortunes.

My fellow storyteller and friend Elizabeth Ellis asks an invaluable question: With all the many stories about Jack, how come there is not one about his mother, whom he left at home? She wrote a poem where she is the mother that watches Jack, a part of her, leave. In this spirit, I write a poem about my search to know Jack.

Knowing Jack

Some say, you don't know Jack.
But I do.
I know him from the rich tales of West Virginia on an old couch
where I learned that the hills mean so much more than hills.

I am a student of Jack, even when I didn't know his name
shouted as Anansi, Hans, Brer, or even Dad.

I know him,
from the ever so tall teller at Kent State
who startling me with the punch of a folktale
or the quiet teller
who reminded me of the value of silence and listening,

Listening deep to the sound that you don't hear unless you pay
attention to it.

Each year, his northwest wind and bean tree move
closer to me.

While in this dance known as storytelling,
I struggle to know me and Jack.

But in the struggle, the story is revealed.

Climbing the stalk not to forget that the tales are as
important as the teaching.
The wind does not blow to separate the two
but instead to start a journey
to understanding
how wind does not work without air.

Breathing in. As teller, as teacher, as listener.
Finding Jack with each exhale, inhale, breath.

I have seen Jack in the eastern hills of Tennessee
In the hijinks and highlights of voices lost and then found.

Wrestling with him in Jonesboro as Hicks brought him to me.
Him arriving on a Ray of sunshine from the Beech mountains.

Invisible he was, when I entered my first classroom,
but he was there. Still is. Working hard to remember that.

He hid in the pages of Chaucer and Shakespeare and even in
the conjugation of verbs. Most of all, in the longing of my students
to tell about them, with them, for them.

He needed helpers and so did I.

I found them in
the voices that we raised together.
Still finding those voices.

From the high school doors to the sometimes stubborn
doors of the academy, he was and still is there.

Sometimes as I stand in the middle, he is always at the center.
To guide me, remind me, even though I left my mama,
she is there, my father too.
My folks bring my lessons to
life.

Whether it is a college or cabin door, Jack is there.
I need to tell his story in order to tell mine.

As I do,
I find Jack and discover new fortunes along the way.

REFERENCES

Adler, P. A., and Adler, P. (1994). "Observational Techniques." In N. K. Denzin and Y. S. Lincoln (Eds.), *Handbook of Qualitative Research* (377–92). Thousand Oaks, CA: Sage.

Agar, M. (2005). "Telling It like You Think It Might Be: Narrative, Linguistic Anthropology, and the Complex Organization." *E:CO* 7 (3–4): 23–34.

Allen, Mitch. Personal interview, May 4, 2006.

Anzaldua, G. E. (1999). *Borderlands/La Frontera: The New Mestiza.* San Francisco: Aunt Lute Books.

Argyris, C., and Schön, D. (1974). *Theory in Practice.* San Francisco: Jossey-Bass.

Babock, B. (1980). "Reflexivity: Definitions and Discriminations." *Semiotica* 30 (1–2): 1–14.

Baker, A., and Greene, E. (1977). *Storytelling: Art and Technique.* New York: Bowker.

Bakhtin, M. (1981). *The Dialogic Imagination: Four Essays.* (Trans.) Michael Holquist and Caryl Emerson. Austin: University of Texas Press (originally published 1975).

Barthes, R. (1987) *Criticism and Truth,* translated and edited by Katrine Pilcher Keunuman. London: Athlone.

Barthes, R. (1974). *S/Z.* (R. Miller, Trans). London: Blackwell.

Barton, B., and Booth, D. (1990). *Stories in the Classroom.* Portsmouth, NH: Heinemann.

Bauman, R. (1978). *Verbal Art as Performance.* Rowley, MA: Newbury House.

Bauman, R., and Sherzer, J. (1975). "The Ethnography of Speaking." *Annual Review of Anthropology* 4 (1): 95–119.

Baumeister, R. F., and Muraven, M. (1996). "Identity as Adaptation to Social, Cultural and Historical Context." *Journal of Adolescence* 19: 405–16.

Baumeister, R. F., and Newman, L. S. (1994). "How Stories Make Sense of Personal Experiences: Motives That Shape Autobiographical Narratives." *Personality and Social Psychology Bulletin* 20 (6): 676–90.

Beach, R., and Myers, J. (2001). *Inquiry-Based English Instruction: Engaging Students in Life and Literature.* New York: Teachers College Press.

Becker, H. S. (2007). *Writing for Social Scientists, 2d edition*. University of Chicago Press.

Behar, R. (1996). *The Vulnerable Observer: Anthropology That Breaks Your Heart*. Boston: Beacon Press.

Benjamin, W. (1969). "The Storyteller: Observations on the Works of Nikolai Leskov." In *Illuminations* (Ed. Hannah Arendt, trans. Harry Zohn). New York: Schoken Books.

Bochner, A. P., and Ellis, C. (2002). *Ethnographically Speaking: Autoethnography, Literature, and Aesthetics*. Walnut Creek, CA: Alta Mira Press.

Bolton, G. M. (2003). *Dorothy Heathcote's Story: Biography of a Remarkable Drama Teacher*. Stoke-on-Trent, UK; Sterling, VA: Trentham Books.

Bolton, G. (1999). *Acting in Classroom Drama*, Portland, ME: Calendar Island.

Bolton, G. M. (1998). *Acting in Classroom Drama: A Critical Analysis*, Birmingham: University of Central England.

Bolton, G. M. (1992). *New Perspectives on Classroom Drama*. London: Simon and Schuster.

Bolton, G. M. (1979). *Toward a Theory of Drama in Education*. London: Longman.

Bolton, G. M., and Heathcote, D. (1999). *So You Want to Use Role-Play?* London: Trentham.

Bolton, G. M., Davis, D., and Lawrence, C. (1986). *Gavin Bolton—Selected Writings*. London; New York: Longman.

Boochner, A. (2001). "Narrative Virtues." *Qualitative Inquiry* 7 (2): 131–57.

Booth, D. (2005). *Story Drama: Creating Stories through Role Playing, Improvising, and Reading Aloud* (2nd ed.). Markham, ON: Pembroke Publishers.

Booth, D. (1994). *Storydrama: Reading, Writing and Role Playing across the Curriculum*. Markham, Ontario: Pembroke.

Booth, D. and Barton, B. (2000). *Storyworks*. Markham, ON: Pembroke.

Booth, D. W., and Lundy, C. J. (1985). *Improvisation: Learning through Drama*. Toronto: Harcourt Canada. 8 ½ x 11 spiral bound.

Bowell, P., and Heap, B. (2001). *Planning Process Drama*. London: David Fulton.

Bruner, J. (2002). *Making Stories. Law, Literature, Life*. Cambridge, MA: Harvard University Press.

Bruner, J. (1996). *The Culture of Education*. Cambridge, MA: Harvard University Press.

Bruner, J. S. (1994). "Life as Narrative." In A. H. Dyson and C. Genishi (Eds.), *The Need for Story: Cultural Diversity in Classroom and Community* (28–37). Urbana, IL: National Council of Teachers of English.

Bruner, J. (1991). "The Narrative Construction of Reality." *Critical Inquiry* 18 (1): 1–21.

Bruner, J. (1990). *Acts of Meaning*. Cambridge, MA: Harvard University Press.

Bruner, J. (1986). *Actual Minds, Possible Worlds*. Cambridge, MA: Harvard University Press.

Campano, G. (2007). *Immigrant Students and Literacy: Reading, Writing and Remembering*. New York: Teachers College Press.

Chambers, E. (2000). "Applied Ethnography." In N. K. Denzin and Y. S. Lincoln (eds.) *Handbook of Qualitative Research* (2nd ed., 851–69). Thousand Oaks, CA: Sage.

Clandinin, D. J., and Connelly, F. M. (2000). *Narrative Inquiry: Experience and Story in Qualitative Research* (1st ed.). San Francisco: Jossey-Bass.

Collins, R., and Cooper, P. J. (1997). *The Power of Story: Teaching through Storytelling* (2nd ed.). Scottsdale, AZ: Gorsuch Scarisbrick.

Connelly, F. M., and Clandinin, D. J. (2006). "Narrative inquiry." In J. L. Green, G. Camlilli, and P. Elmore (Eds.), *Handbook of Complementary Methods in Education Research* (3rd ed., 447–87). Mahwah, NJ: Lawrence Erlbaum.

Connelly, F. M., and Clandinin, D. J. (1990). "Stories of Experience and Narrative Inquiry." *Educational Researcher* 19 (5): 2–14.

Creswell, J. W. (2003). *Research Design: Qualitative, Quantitative and Mixed Methods Approaches*. Thousand Oaks, CA: Sage.

Crotty, M. (1998). *The Foundations of Social Research: Meaning and Perspective in the Research Process*. London: Sage.

Cureton, D., and Eldridge, R. (1984). "Teaching Poor Readers in the Regular Classroom." In J. F. Baumann and D. D. Johnson (Eds.), *Reading Instruction and the Beginning Teacher: A Practical Guide*. Minneapolis: Burgess.

Daiute, Colette. (2014). *Narrative Inquiry: A Dynamic Approach*. New York: Sage.

Davis, B., Sumara, D. J., and Luce-Kapler, R. (2008). *Engaging Minds: Changing Teaching in Complex Times* (2nd ed.). New York: Routledge.

Davis, D. (1992). *Southern Jack Tales*. Little Rock, AR: August House.

De Lint, C. (1987). *Jack the Giant Killer*. New York: Ace Books.

Denzin, N., and Lincoln, Y. (Eds.). (1998). *Collecting and Interpreting Qualitative Materials*. Thousand Oaks, CA: Sage.

Denzin, N. K. (1997). *Interpretive Ethnography: Ethnographic Practices for the 21st Century*. Thousand Oaks, CA: Sage.

Denzin, N. K., and Lincoln, Y. S. (2008). *Strategies of Qualitative Inquiry* (3rd ed.). Thousand Oaks, CA: Sage.

Denzin, N. K., and Lincoln, Y. S. (2000). *Handbook of Qualitative Research* (2nd ed.). Thousand Oaks, CA: Sage.

Dewey, J. (1933). *How We Think, a Restatement of the Relation of Reflective Thinking to the Educative Process*. Boston, New York [etc.], DC: Heath.

Diamond, E. (1996). *Performance and Cultural Politics*. New York: Routledge.

Dozier, C., Johnston, P., and Rogers, R. (2006). *Critical Literacy/Critical Teaching: Tools Preparing Responsive Teachers*. New York: Teachers College Press.

Dyer, J., and Keller-Cohen, D. (2000). "The Discursive Construction of Professional Self through Narratives of Personal Experience." *Discourse Studies* 2 (3): 283–304.

Dyson, A. H. (1997). *Writing Superheroes: Contemporary Childhood, Popular Culture, and Classroom Literacy*. Williston, VT: Teachers College Press.

Dyson, A. H., and Genishi, C. (1994). *The Need for Story: Cultural Diversity in Classroom and Community*. Urbana, IL: National Council of Teachers of English.

Edmiston, B. (in revision). "Authoring Complexity in Dialogic Dramatic Inquiry." *Pedagogies: An International Journal*.

Edmiston, B. (2010). "Using Dramatic Inquiry as a Literacy Tool: Imaginative Explorations in Actual Pasts, Lived Presents, and Possible Futures." In R. Beach, G. Campano, M. Borgman, and B. Edmiston (Eds.), *Literacy Tools in 21st Century Classrooms: Unleashing Student Agency*. New York: Teachers College Press.

Edmiston, B. (2008a). *Forming Ethical Identities in Early Childhood Play*. London and New York: Routledge.

Edmiston, B. (2008b). *Mountains, Ships, and Time-Machines: Making Space for Creativity and Learning with Dramatic Inquiry in a Primary Classroom*. Durham, UK: Creative Partnerships.

Edmiston, B. (2007). "Mission to Mars: Using Drama to Make Classrooms More Inclusive for the Language and Literacy Learning of Children with Disabilities." *Language Arts* 84 (4): 331–340.

Edmiston, B. (2003). "What's My position? Role, Frame, and Positioning When Using Process Drama." *Research in Drama Education* 8 (2): 221–29.

Edmiston, B., and Bigler-McCarthy, T. (2006). *Building Social Justice Communities: Using Drama to Make Power More Visible*. http://www.mantleoftheexpert.com/ . . . /Building%20Social%20Justice.pdf.

Edmiston, B., Whittaker, M., Cushman, C. and Ressler, M. (in revision). "Teaching at the Edges When Authoring Is Central: Using Dialogic Dramatic Inquiry to Create More Inclusive Anti-oppressive Classroom Authoring Spaces." *Journal of Early Childhood Literacy*.

Edwards, D., and Mercer, N. (1987). *Common Knowledge: The Development of Understanding in the Classroom*. London: Routledge.

Egan, K. (1989). *Teaching as Storytelling: An Alternative Approach to Teaching and Curriculum in the Elementary School*. Chicago: University of Chicago Press.

Eisner, E. W. (1991). *The Enlightened Eye: Qualitative Inquiry and the Enhancement of Educational Practice.* New York: Macmillan.

Elliott, J. (2005). *Using Narrative in Social Research: Qualitative and Quantitative Approaches.* Thousand Oaks, CA: Sage.

Ellis, C. (1999). "Heartful Autoethnography." *Qualitative Health Research* 9 (5): 669–83.

Ellis, C. (1997) "Evocative Autoethnography: Writing Emotionally about Our Lives." In W. G. Tierney and Y. S. Lincoln (Eds.), *Representation and Text: Reframing the Narrative Voice.* New York: State University of New York Press.

Ellis C., and Bochner, A. P. (2006). "Analyzing Analytic Autoethnography: An Autopsy." *Journal of Contemporary Ethnography* 35: 429–49.

Emerson, R. M., Fretz, R. I., and Shaw, L. L. (1995). *Writing Ethnographic Fieldnotes.* Chicago: University of Chicago Press.

Forest, H. (2008). *The Inside Story: An Arts-based Exploration of the Creative Process of the Storyteller as Leader.* Yellow Springs, Antioch University.

Foucault, M. (1976). *Mental Illness and Psychology* (1st ed.). New York: Harper and Row.

Freire, P. (2007). *Pedagogy of the Oppressed.* New York: Continuum.

Freire, P. (1970). *Pedagogy of the Oppressed.* New York: Seabury.

Geertz, C. (1973). *Thick Description: Toward an Interpretive Theory of Culture; the Interpretation of Culture.* New York: Basic Books.

Georgakopoulou, A. (2006). "Small and Large Identities in Narrative (Inter)-Action." In A. De Fina, D. Schiffrin, and M. Bamberg (Eds.), *Discourse and Identity.* Cambridge, UK: Cambridge University Press.

Gergen, M., and Gergen, K. (2002). "Ethnographic Representation as Relationship." In A. Bochner and C. Ellis (Eds.), *Ethnographically Speaking: Autoethnography, Literature, and Aesthetics.* Walnut Creek, CA: Altamira, 11–33.

Gillard, M. (1996). *Storyteller, Storyteacher: Discovering the Power of Storytelling for Teaching and Living.* York, ME: Stenhouse.

Goffman, E. (1974). *Frame Analysis: An Essay on the Organization of Experience.* New York: Harper and Row.

Goldblatt, E., and Smith, M. W. (1995). *Alone with Each Other: Conceptions of Discussion in One College Classroom Community.* Linguistics and Education 7, 327–48.

Goldblatt, E. C. (1995). *'Round My Way: Authority and Double-Consciousness in Three Urban High School Writers.* Pittsburgh: University of Pittsburgh Press.

Goodman, K. S. (1989). "Whole-Language Research: Foundations and Development." *The Elementary School Journal* 90: 207–20.

Greene, M. (1973). *Teacher as Stranger: Educational Philosophy for the Modern Age.* Belmont, CA: Wadsworth.

Gudmundsdottir, S. (1995). "The Narrative Nature of Pedagogical Content Knowledge." In H. McEwan and K. Egan (Eds.), *Narrative in Teaching, Learning, and Research.* New York: Teacher's College, Columbia University.

Guralnik, D. B. (1982). (Ed.). *Webster's New World Dictionary.* New York: Simon and Schuster.

Hardy, B. (1978). "Towards a Poetics of Fiction: An Approach through Narrative" In M. Meek, A. Warlow, and G. Barton (Eds.), *The Cool Web.* New York: Antheneum.

Hargreaves, A., Earl, L., and Ryan, J. (1996). *Schooling for Change.* London: Falmer.

Hayano, D. (1979). "Auto-Ethnography: Paradigms, Problems, and Prospects." *Human Organization* 38 (1): 99–104.

Heathcote, D. (2006). Personal interview.

Heathcote, D. (1984). *Dorothy Heathcote: Collected Writings on Education and Drama.* Eds. Liz Johnson and Cecily O'Neill. Essex: D. P. Media Limited.

Heathcote, D. (1978). "Excellence in Teaching—Collected Writings on Education and Drama." New Zealand journal *Education.*

Heathcote, D., and Bolton, G. M. (1995). *Drama for Learning: Dorothy Heathcote's "Mantle of the Expert" Approach to Education.* Portsmouth, NH: Heinemann.

Heathcote, D., Johnson, L., and O'Neill, C. (1984). *Dorothy Heathcote: Collected Writings of Education and Drama.* London: Hutchinson.

Hicks, O. (2009). *Jack Tales and Mountain Yarns: As Told by Orville Hicks.* Boone, NC: Parkway.

Holland, D., Lachiotte, W., Skinner, D., and Cain, C. (1998). *Identity and Agency in Cultural Worlds.* Cambridge, MA: Harvard University Press.

Holman Jones, S., with Bell, E. (2008). "Performing Resistance." In E. Bell, *Theories of Performance: Selves, Scenes, Screens* (199–232). Thousand Oaks, CA: Sage. *Journal of Health Care for the Poor and Underserved* 19 (3): 1010–11.

Johnson, L., and O'Neill, C. (1984) *Dorothy Heathcote: Collected Writings on Education and Drama.* London: Hutchinson.

Jones, K. (2008). "Narrative Matters: The Power of the Personal Essay in Health Policy." *Journal of Health Care for the Poor and Underserved* 19 (3): 1011–13.

Jones, S. H., Adams, T. E., and Ellis, C. (Eds.). (2013). "Coming to Know Autoethnogrpahy as More than a Method." In *Handbook of Autoethnography.* Walnut Creek, CA: Left Coast.

Jorgensen, D. L. (1989). *Participant Observation: A Methodology for Human Studies.* Newbury Park, CA: Sage.

Josselson, R. (2006). "Narrative Research and the Challenge of Accumulating Knowledge." *Narrative Inquiry* 16 (1): 3–10.

Jungk, S. (2001). "How Does It Matter? Teacher Inquiry in the Tradition of Social Science Research." In G. Burnaford, J. Fischert, and D. Hobson (Eds.), *Teachers Doing Research* (2nd ed.). Mahwah, NJ: Erlbaum.

Keller-Cohen, D., and Dyer, J. (2000). "The Discursive Construction of Professional Self through Narratives of Personal Experience." https://www .researchgate.net/journal/1461-4456_Discourse Studies 2 (3): 283–304.

Keller-Cohen, D., and Dyer, J. (1997). "Intertextuality and the Narrative of Personal Experience." *Journal of Narrative and Life History* 7 (1–4): 147–53.

Kemmis, S. (1985). "Action Research and the Politics of Reflection." In D. Boud, R. Keogh, and D. Walker (Eds.), *Reflection: Turning Experience into Learning* (139–63). London: Kogan Page.

Kentner, M. G. (2013). Personal interview.

Kim, J. (2016). *Understanding Narrative Inquiry.* Thousand Oaks, CA: Sage.

King, N. (1993). *Storymaking and Drama: An Approach to Teaching Language and Literature at the Secondary and Postsecondary Levels.* Portsmouth, NH: Heinemann.

Kottkamp, R. B. (February 1990). "Means for Facilitating Reflection." *Education and Urban Society,* 22: 182–203.

Labov, W. (1972). *Language in the Inner City: Study in the Black English Vernacular.* Philadelphia: University of Pennsylvania Press.

Ladson-Billings, G. J. (2001). *Crossing over to Canaan: The Journey of New Teachers in Diverse Classrooms.* San Francisco, CA: Jossey-Bass.

Langellier, K., and Peterson, E. E. (2004). *Storytelling in Daily Life: Performing Narrative.* Philadelphia: Temple University Press.

LeCompte, M. D. and Goetz, J. P. (1982). "Problems of Reliability and Validity in Ethnographic Research." *Review of Educational Research* 51: 31–60.

Lichtman, M. (2006). *Qualitative Research in Education: A User's Guide.* Thousand Oaks, CA: Sage.

Lincoln, Y., and Guba, E. (1985). *Naturalistic Inquiry.* New York: Sage.

Lindahl, C. (2001). *Perspectives on the Jack Tales and Other North American Marchen.* Bloomington: Indiana University Press.

Lindahl, C. (1994). "Jack: The Name, the Tales, the American Tradition." In *Jack in Two Worlds.* Chapel Hill: University of North Carolina Press.

Lipman, D. (1999). *Improving Your Storytelling: Beyond the Basics for All Who Tell Stories in Work or Play.* Little Rock, AR: August House.

Lynd, H. M. 1961 [1958]. *On Shame and the Search for Identity.* New York: Science Editions.

Mattingly, C. (1991). "Narrative Reflections on Practical Actions: Two Learning Experiments in Reflective Storytelling." In D. A. Schön (Ed.), *The Reflective*

Turn: Case Studies in and on Educational Practice (235–57). New York: Teachers College Press.

Mattson, C., and Tatar, M. (2016). "Fairytales, Myth, Fantasy." In C. Schwabe and C. Jones, *New Approaches Teaching Folk and Fairytales*. Louisville: University Press of Colorado.

McCarthy, W., and Stotter, R. (1994). "The Tellers and the Tales: Revivalist Storytelling." In William McCarthy (Ed.), *Jack in Two Worlds: Contemporary North American Tales and the Tellers* (153–67). Chapel Hill: University of North Carolina Press.

McCaleb, S. P. (1994). *Building Communities of Learners: Collaboration among Teachers, Students, Families, and Community*. New York: St. Martin's.

McCaslin, N. (1996). *Creative Drama in the Classroom and Beyond* (6th ed.). New York: Longman.

McEwan, H. (1995). "Narrative Understanding in the Study of Teaching." In H. McEwan and K. Egan (Eds.), *Narrative in Teaching, Learning, and Research* (166–83). New York: Teachers College Press.

Merriam, S. B., and Associates (2002). *Qualitative Research in Practice: Examples for Discussion and Analysis*. San Francisco: Jossey-Bass.

Mills, M. A. (1990). *Oral Narrative in Afghanistan: The Individual in Tradition*. New York: Garland.

Moffett, J. (1983). *Teaching the Universe of Discourse*. Boston: Houghton Mifflin.

Mora, P. (1993). *Nepantla: Essays of the Land in the Middle*. Albuquerque: University of New Mexico Press.

Mora, P., McKnight, D., Ceballos, J., and López, A. (1993). *Qué dice el desierto?* Boston: Houghton Mifflin.

Morris, W. (Ed.). (2002). *The American Heritage College Dictionary* (4th ed.). Boston: Houghton Mifflin.

Neelands, J. (2009). "Acting Together: Ensemble as a Democratic Process in Art and Life." *Research in Drama Education: The Journal of Applied Theatre and Performance* 14 (2): 173–89.

Neelands, J. (1984). *Making Sense of Drama*. Heinemann: London.

Neelands, J., and Goode, T. (2000). *Structuring Drama Work: A Handbook of Available Forms in Theatre and Drama*. Cambridge, UK: Cambridge University Press.

Nelson, H. L. (2001). *Damaged Identity, Narrative Repair*. Ithaca: Cornell University Press.

Nightingale, D., and Cromby, J. (Eds.). 1999. *Social Constructionist Psychology: A Critical Analysis of Theory and Practice*. Buckingham: Open University Press.

Noddings, N., and Shore, P. J. (1998). *Awakening the Inner Eye: Intuition in Education*. Troy, NY: Educator's International.

Norfolk, B., and Norfolk, S. (1999). *The Moral of the Story: Folktales for Character Development*. Little Rock, AR: August House.

Norrick, Neal R. (2007). "Conversational Storytelling." In D. Herman (Ed.), *The Cambridge Companion to Narrative* (127–41). Cambridge: Cambridge University Press.

Norrick, N. R. (2000a). "Conversational Narrative: Storytelling in Everyday Talk." *Current Issues in Linguistic Theory* 203: 233.

Norrick, N. R. (2000b). *Conversational Narrative*. Amsterdam: Benjamins.

Norrick, N. R. (2000/2001). "Poetics and Conversation." *Connotations* 10 (2–3): 243–67.

Nyabadza, G. W. (2003, June 20). "Leadership at the Peak—Africa Needs Dedicated Leaders." Africa News Service. Retrieved from *Expanded Academic ASAP Plus*.

Oakes, J., and Lipton, M. (2003). *Teaching to Change the World*. Boston: McGraw-Hill.

Ochs, E., and Capps, L. (2001). *Living Narrative: Creating Lives in Everyday Storytelling*. Cambridge, MA: Harvard University Press.

O'Neill, C. (1995). *Drama Worlds: A Framework for Process Drama*. Portsmouth, NH: Heinemann.

O'Neill, C., and Lambert, A. (1984). *Drama Structures: A Practical Handbook for Teachers*. London: Hutchinson.

O'Neill, C., and Lambert, A. (1982). *Drama Structures: A Practical Handbook for Teachers*. Gloucester: Stanley Thornes.

Oring, E. (1994). "The Arts, Artifacts and Artifices of Identity." *Journal of American Folklore* 107: 211–47.

Pagnucci, G. S. (2004). *Living the Narrative Life: Stories as a Tool for Meaning Making*. Portsmouth, NH: Boynton/Cook.

Paley, V. G. (1990). *The Boy Who Would Be a Helicopter*. Cambridge, MA: Harvard University Press.

Pavesic, C. (2005). *Ray Hicks and the Jack Tales*. iUniverse.

Pepper, K., and Thomas, L. (2002). "Making a Change: The Effects of the Leadership Role on School Climate." *Learning Environments Research* 5 (2): 155–66.

Perdue, C. L. (2001). *Is Old Jack Really Richard Chase? Perspectives on the Jack Tales and Other North American Marchen*. Bloomington: Indiana University Press.

Perdue, C. L., Jr. (Ed.). *Outwitting the Devil: Jack Tales from Wise County Virginia*. New Mexico: Ancient City, 1987.

Phillips, C., and Tatar, M. (2016). *Fairy Tales, Myth, and Fantasy, New Approaches to Teaching Folk and Fairy Tales*. Boulder: University Press of Colorado.

Pinar, W. F. (2017). "That First Year." *Currere Exchange Journal* 1 (1): 1–10.

Polakow, V. (1985). "Whose Stories Should We Tell? A Call to Action." *Language Arts* 62 (8): 826–35.

Polkinghorne, D. (1988). *Narrative Knowing and the Human Sciences*. Albany: State University of New York Press.

Pratt, M. L. (2008). *Imperial Eyes: Travel Writing and Transculturation* (2nd ed.). London; New York: Routledge.

Qualley, D. (1997). *Turns of Thought: Teaching Composition as Reflexive Inquiry*. Portsmouth, NH: Heinemann Boynton/Cook.

Reed-Danahay, D. E. (1997). "Introduction." In Reed-Danahay (Ed.), *Auto/Ethnography: Rewriting the Self and the Social*. Oxford: Berg.

Rehak, Jay (2008). "Go Back and Circle the Verbs." In Rick Ayers and Patricia Ford (Eds.), *City Kids, City Teachers: Reports from the Front Row*. New York: New Press.

Ress, R. (2007). *Tangora* magazine, http://reginaress.com/articles/the-storytelling-revival-in-the-united-states.

Richardson, L. (2000a). "New Writing Practices in Qualitative Research." *Sociology of Sport Journal*, 17: 5–20.

Richardson, L. (2000b). "Writing: A Method of Inquiry." In N. K. Denzin and Y. S. Lincoln (Eds.), *Handbook of Qualitative Research* (2nd ed., 923–48). Thousand Oaks, CA: Sage.

Richardson, L. (1997). *Fields of Play: Constructing an Academic Life*. New Brunswick, NJ: Rutgers University Press.

Rosen, B. (1988). *And None of It Was Nonsense: The Power of Storytelling in School*. Portsmouth, NH: Heinemann.

Rosen, H. (March, 1986). "The Importance of Story." *Language Arts* 63 (3): 226–37.

Roth, W. M. (2008). (Ed.). Auto/Biography and Auto/Ethnography: Praxis of Research Method.

Ryan, M-L. (2004) *Narrative across Media* (Lincoln, London: University of Nebraska Press).

Sadker, M., and Sadker, D. M. (1994). *Failing at Fairness: How America's Schools Cheat Girls*. New York: C. Scribner.

Salsi, L. (2000). *The Jack Tales: Stories by Ray Hicks*. New York: Callway.

Salverson, J. (2001). "Change on Whose Terms? Testing an Erotic of Inquiry." *Theater* 3 (3): 119–25.

Sawyer, R. (1962, revised, 1942). *The Way of the Storyteller*. New York: Viking.

Schön, D. A. (1983). *The Reflective Practitioner: How Professionals Think in Action.* London: Temple Smith.

Schubert, W. H. (1991). "Teacher Lore: A Basis for Understanding Praxis." In C. Witherell and N. Noddings (Eds.), *Stories Lives Tell: Narrative and Dialogue in Education* (207–33). New York: Teachers College Press.

Scott, D., and Morrison, M. (2007). *Key Ideas in Educational Research.* London: Continuum.

Shank, G. D. (2002). *Qualitative Research: A Personal Skills Approach.* Columbus, OH: Merrill Prentice Hall.

Short, K., and Harste, J., with Burke, C. (1996). *Creating Classrooms for Authors and Inquirers.* Portsmouth, NH: Heinemann.

Shuman, A. (2005). *Other People's Stories: Entitlement Claims and the Critique of Empathy.* Urbana: University of Illinois Press.

Shuman, A. (1986). *Storytelling Rights: The Uses of Oral and Written Texts by Urban Adolescents.* Cambridge [Cambridgeshire]; New York: Cambridge University Press.

Smith, G. 2006. *Erving Goffman.* New York: Routledge.

Sobol, J. (1999). *The Storytellers' Journey: An American Revival.* Chicago, University of Illinois Press.

Sobol, J. (1992). "Introduction." In D. Davis, *Southern Jack Tales.* Little Rock: August House.

Sparkes, A. C. (2001) "Autoethnography: Self-indulgence or Something More?" In A. Bochner and C. Ellis (Eds.), *Ethnographically Speaking: Autoethnography, Literature, and Aesthetics.* Walnut Creek, CA: Alta Mira.

Spry, T. (2001). "Performing Autoethnography: An Embodied Methodological Praxis." *Qualitative Inquiry* 7 (6): 706–32.

Stake, R. E. (1988). "Case Study Methods in Educational Research: Making Sweet Water." In R. M. Jaegar (Ed.), *Complementary Methods for Research in Education* (253–65). Washington, DC: American Educational Research Association.

Stone, K. (1997). "Social Identity in Organized Storytelling." *Western Folklore* 56: 234.

Stone, K. F. (1998). *Burning Brightly: New Light on Old Tales Told Today.* Peterborough, ON; Orchard Park, NY: Broadview.

Stotter, R., and McCarthy, W. (2010) *The Tellers and the Tales: Revivalist Storytelling, Jack in Two Worlds.* Chapel Hill: University of North Carolina Press.

Strum, B. (2000). "The Storylistening Trance Experience." *Journal of American Folklore* 113: 287–304.

Taylor, P., and Warner, C. (November 2004). *Structure and Spontaneity: Selected Writings on Drama and Education by Cecily O'Neill*. Oakhill, Stoke-on-Trent, UK: Trentham Books.

Taylor, P., and Warner, C. D. (2006). *Structure and Spontaneity: The Process Drama of Cecily O'Neill*. Stoke on Trent, UK; Sterling, USA: Trentham.

Tierney, W. G. (2002). "Get Real: Representing Reality." *Qualitative Studies in Education* 15: 385–98.

Tierney, W. G. (1998). "Life History's History: Subjects Foretold." *Sociology* 27: 41–52.

Tierney, W. G., and Lincoln, Y. S. (Eds.). (1997). *Representation and the Text: Reframing the Narrative Voice*. Albany: State University of New York Press.

Vygotsky, L. (1978). "Problems of Method." In *Mind in Society* (52–75). (Trans. M. Cole). Cambridge, MA: Harvard University Press.

Wagner, B. J. (1976). *Dorothy Heathcote: Drama as a Learning Medium*. Washington, DC: National Education Association.

Wagner, B. J. (Ed.). (1998). *Educational Drama and Language Arts: What Research Shows*. Portsmouth, NH: Heinemann.

Ware, P. D. (2006). "From Sharing Time to Showtime: Valuing Diverse Venues for Storytelling in Technology-rich Classrooms." *Language Arts* 84 (1): 45–54.

Welty, E. (1984). *One Writer's Beginnings*. On Massey lectures 1983 [sound recording] Cambridge, Mass.: Harvard University Press.

Wilhelm, J. D., and Edmiston, B. (1998). *Imagining to Learn, Inquiry, Ethics and Integration through Drama*. Portsmouth, NH: Heinemann.

Williamson, D. and Williamson, L. (2011). *Jack and the Devil's Purse: Scottish Traveller Tales*. Edinburgh: Birlinn.

Winn, R. B. (1960). *A Concise Dictionary of Existentialism*. New York: Philosophical Library.

Wolf, E. (Producer) (2010, November 30) Interview with Octavia Sexton (Audio Podcast). Retrieved from http://www.artofstorytellingshow.com/2010/11/30/octavia-sexton-jack-story-traditional-tale/.

Wolf, S. A. (2004). *Interpreting Literature with Children*. Mahwah, NJ: Lawrence Erlbaum.

Wolf, S. A., and Enciso, P. (1994). "Multiple Selves in Literary Interpretation: Engagement and the Language of Drama." In D. J. Leu and C. K. Kinzer (Eds.), *Multidimensional Aspects of Literacy Research, Theory, and Practice: Forty-Third Yearbook of the National Reading Conference* (351–60). Chicago, IL: National Reading Conference.

Witherell, Carol and Noddings, Nel (Eds.). (1991). *Stories Lives Tell*. New York: Teachers College Press.

Zipes, J. (2012). *The Irresistible Fairy Tale: The Cultural and Societal History of a Genre*. Princeton: Princeton University Press.

INDEX

www.ingramcontent.com/pod-product-compliance
Lightning Source LLC
Chambersburg PA
CBHW031129270326
41929CB00011B/1558